Dog Training
The Gentle Modern Method

David Weston

Dog Training

The Gentle Modern Method

HOWELL
BOOK HOUSE

New York

Howell Book House
A Simon & Schuster Macmillan Company
1633 Broadway
New York, NY 10019

Library of Congress Cataloging-in-Publication Data

Weston, David.
    Dog training: the gentle modern method / David Weston. — 1st
Howell Book House ed.
        p.   cm.
    ISBN 0-87605-511-0
    1. Dogs—Training. I. Title.
SF431.W47   1992   91-45377   CIP
636.7'088'7—dc20

First Howell Book House Edition 1992
10 9 8

Printed in Hong Kong

FOREWORD

I have been involved in the teaching of clinical veterinary medicine to students for over twenty years. The training that a veterinarian receives necessarily concentrates on the recognition and management of physical disease in the domestic species and only touches peripherally on animal behaviour and the psychology of the animal–human relationship.

However, all too often in our contact with animal patients for medical problems, we observe behaviour in the animal that reflects inappropriate or inadequate training of the animal. Such behaviour makes it difficult for us as veterinarians to do a proper job of examining and treating these patients, and is a source of embarrassment and frustration to the animal's owner.

To help me deal with some of these problems, I have been fortunate enough to be able to refer to an expert animal behaviourist and dog trainer, David Weston, who has produced this excellent manual.

David has given a number of lectures and demonstrations to our students and staff, and has shown to us a method of training that is so rapid, effective and obviously enjoyable for the dog, that one is easily convinced of its correctness. David's methods have been developed from established scientific data on canine behaviour, backed up by his keen observation and a gentle, confident and caring approach to the task. Such is the effectiveness of David's method that an untrained pup can be taught to come, sit and stand in less than a minute. His gentle attitude to training carries through to his general philosophy of the role of dogs in our society.

Australia has one of the highest levels of pet ownership in the world, and apart from concerning ourselves with our animal companions' physical health, it is a part of responsibile pet ownership to ensure that our dogs are socially acceptable and able to cope with living and interacting with man in the modern urban environment. Proper training is an essential part of that responsibility. I can recommend David Weston's training methods as simple, quick, effective and above all, enjoyable for both trainer and dog.

March 1990

R. W. Mitten, BVSc
Lecturer in Small Animal Medicine
School of Veterinary Medicine
University of Melbourne

ACKNOWLEDGMENTS

Giving credit where credit is due presents no difficulty for me in regards to the time, effort and support I received whilst compiling this book.

It is simply a statement of fact that without the constructive input and encouragement from Ruth Ross this book would never have seen the printer's ink.

My thanks go to Joy Ryan in appreciation of her typing skills and to my friend Colin Lampshire for the many hours spent on his computer producing the final copies of the manuscript.

The publisher, Anne Godden suggested many pertinent changes which made the book easier to understand and more enjoyable to read.

I am grateful to all those who made themselves available for photography, and to the past and present members of The Kintala Club who presented me with a myriad of canine interactions at their training sessions, from which I gleaned so much knowledge.

CONTENTS

Dedication

'FRED'

HAD HE NOT COME INTO MY LIFE AND FILLED
ME WITH HIS PRESENCE I DOUBT WHETHER THE
METHOD OR THIS BOOK WOULD EVER HAVE
EVENTUATED

INTRODUCTION

Turning back the clock to my childhood, I recall that my home always resounded to the chatter of a pet budgerigar or the patter of feet belonging to either a dog or a cat. When I was ten years old, I was given my first dog, a wirehaired terrier whom I called Asta. Dog training schools were virtually unheard of in England in the 1940s, so I set about the task of teaching my pal some exercises in my own boyish way. The exercises were mostly game orientated such as retrieving, hide and seek, rolling over, or jumping into my arms. These early experiences must have made an unconscious but lasting impression on my future attitude towards animals and their training. Without giving any real consideration to the consequences of my methods of teaching, it nevertheless imprinted in my mind the idea that dogs could be taught to respond voluntarily and without threat or punishment.

Approximately twenty years later I came to Australia and settled in the town of Montmorency in Victoria. In 1966 I acquired 'Fred', a Miniature Schnauzer puppy. Little did I realise the impact he was going to make on my life. When he reached six months of age, I took him to a nearby dog obedience club.

During the next few years, I worked hard at learning and applying the knowledge which the club had to offer, and as a consequence I became a Kennel Control Council certified instructor, a full panel obedience judge and President of the Club. During this period Fred gained his Companion Dog (C.D.) and Companion Dog Excellent (C.D.X.) titles. However, I became increasingly disenchanted with the method of training used by dog clubs in general. Much of the knowledge that supported their method appeared to be based on archaic principles and involve a great deal of punishment and compulsion. Training essentially consisted of jerking the dog in the neck with a choker chain, physically pressuring it into position, and growling at the dog using commanding voice tones. When the dog responded in a way which was favourable to the handler it was rewarded with a pat and verbal praise. Many of the responses generated were accompanied by a strong fear reaction in the dogs, as could be seen by the lowering of their ears and tails, and an unwillingness to return voluntarily to the handlers.

I began to remember my childhood experiences and my resentment of the compulsive method of training used by obedience clubs gradually overwhelmed me. I searched amongst many dog training books for information that would support the views I had developed as a boy. Unfortunately they more or less endorsed the principles which I was learning vehemently to oppose.

Quite by chance, I came across a reference to a man who had trained rats, Professor B. F. Skinner, one of the most influential behaviourists alive today. His experiments with rats in the 1930s led him to develop a theory on the learning process in animals to which he gave the scientific name of 'operant conditioning'. I eagerly collected and read as many of his books and articles as possible. As I read, I became more and more certain that I had found what I was looking for. Skinner had proved that rats and other animals could be taught to perform a series of complex actions in order to obtain the benefit of a piece of food. Most importantly, he did this without employing any force or punishment.

It became a challenge for me to understand Skinner's theories, so that I could develop a way of using them to teach dogs. I was fortunate in that a number of wandering dogs liked to visit my property. I practised my new found theories on them and was astounded by the speed at which they learnt their exercises. Furthermore, although I did not see some dogs for weeks after their initial training, when they returned, they had remembered most of their lessons.

A funny thing happened! Whenever I took Fred for a walk, I used to gather many of these dogs around me like the Pied Piper and it was not unusual for half a dozen dogs to share the pleasures of a bush walk with Fred and me.

I was already excited by the progress I had made in dog psychology. However, there were more revelations to come.

I did not know very much about a dog's natural behaviour I realised and I set out to learn more. I wanted to find out why dogs behave the way they do. I studied the make-up and behaviour of the wolf as this animal is now acknowledged to be the direct ancestor of the dog, and found the answers to many of the questions I had been asking.

Why, for instance, does a dog respond more readily to something moving close to the ground than to things above its head?

Why is a dog more likely to investigate something emitting a high pitched sound than a low harsh noise?

The more I found out, the more things seemed to fit into place.

It makes me sad that dogs in their countless thousands are still being trained with the old compulsive method and subjected to the misinformation and attitudes that go with it and I hope this book will change this and, as a consequence, more people will understand and appreciate their dogs.

March 1990   *David Weston*

CHAPTER *1* THE SENSES

In order to communicate with dogs and understand how they learn, we must first know something about their senses, how they see, hear, touch, taste and smell. We can then make our dogs respond to us in a way which suits their physical abilities and which is similar to the way in which they would survive in a natural environment.

Experts are agreed that *canis familiaris* (the domestic dog) evolved from various types of *canis lupus* (the wolf) throughout many parts of the world. In approximately twelve thousand years, humans have bred dogs into the many shapes and sizes that we see today. However, the behaviour of all our domestic dogs is very much the same as their wild ancestors. If they were left alone the changes to their behaviour which we have engineered would soon disappear. For example, a pointer would not point for long if it was extremely hungry. It would quickly be stimulated to kill. Likewise, a retriever would not bring back food for others to eat, it would eat it itself! So, when you are looking at your dog, you can say you are looking at a wolf in dog's clothing! When we have learnt this, we are in a good position to understand why dogs' senses have developed in the way they have. These senses are all geared to survival in the wild and, although our dogs don't need to hunt for food or to find a mate, the ability to do so in most breeds is apparent to anyone who has observed dog behaviour.

The sense of sight

Without good eyesight a dog would not survive for long in the wild. Like humans, its sense of sight is stimulated continually while it is awake. The anatomy and position of its eye, if compared with the human eye, gives a more limited binocular vision, poor colour reception and an inferior awareness of detail. Hardly qualities consistent with survival! However, these deficiencies are more than adequately compensated for by the set of their eyes which gives them an extra-ordinary ability to notice the slightest movement over a wide area. They are interested in other ground running animals rather than tree-dwelling creatures, because it is easier for them to kill animals on the ground. Most dogs are not interested in birds in trees, aeroplanes, telegraph wires or other objects which they can't reach. However, they react immediately to movement at ground level.

TRAINING IMPLICATIONS

1. Hand signals made at waist level or lower will attract more attention than those made above the head.
2. Moving hand signals will elicit more interest and action in the dog.
3. Alterations to hand signals however slight will tend to produce different responses in the dog.
4. There are a number of long-haired breeds whose eyesight is hampered by a lot of facial hair. Pinning, clipping or tying back this hair will improve the sight of these dogs.

The sense of hearing

Hearing is measured in cycles per second (c.p.s.) or hertz. The human range is from a base tone of 20 c.p.s. to a high-pitched sound of approximately 20,000 c.p.s. Any sound over 20,000 c.p.s. is referred to as ultrasonic. Dogs can hear noises ranging from 20 c.p.s. to an amazing level of at least 35,000 c.p.s. Again this helps the dogs' survival, for many small animals such as rodents emit ultrasonic sounds and the dog can therefore use its hearing to find a meal!

Dogs learn to locate the source of a sound with great accuracy, using their large mobile ear flaps. Experiments have shown that they are able to pinpoint a sound within five degrees when it is placed anywhere in a circle of 360 degrees. It is interesting to discover how this skill develops by watching puppies at play, and then observing adult dogs. Puppies often look around them in some bewilderment when you call them. It takes them some time to locate you, particularly if you are standing still. The experienced adult dog does not have this problem unless its hearing has deteriorated with age or disease.

TRAINING IMPLICATIONS

Dogs quickly react to high, sharp, sounds such as a gate latch, a key in a lock, or the sound of scissors cutting up slivers of meat. This suggests that dogs will be interested in similar voice signals and will be more likely to respond to them.

1. Dogs will always react to a hissing sound made through the teeth. Saying 'sit' or 'stand' in a similar way will elicit extreme interest.

2. It is always better to use high-pitched voice signals rather than low, commanding ones.
3. When calling a young puppy from a distance, it is better to move away from it while you say 'come', so that it is easier for the puppy to find you.

The sense of smell

The incredible capacity of the dog's sense of smell has been proved by numerous scientific and practical tests. Dogs have been able to find people buried under many feet of snow. They can be trained to detect gas leaks underground, to sniff out drugs, and even to discover when a cow is in season.

Why then do so many dogs who stray become lost, and unable to find their way home?

Wolves provide the answer. In their vast area of almost virgin territory, a wolf is not exposed to human smells, but simply to the trails of other animals. Even a wolf would get lost in suburbia. His sense of smell was not developed to cope with the numerous odours created by human beings and their urban lifestyle.

Nevertheless, dogs, like wolves, will demonstrate their remarkable scenting abilities when it comes to finding food. Wandering dogs easily hone in on rubbish bins! Food left in an accessible place around the house or the garden will quickly disappear — and we know where! Take a dog for a walk in the bush and it will invariably find some dead animal.

TRAINING IMPLICATIONS

The wolf and the dog are both predisposed to think about food and use their sense of smell to find it. This strong instinct can be used in the training of dogs.

The sense of touch

Human beings pat dogs basically for three reasons. Firstly, for the pleasure that stroking a warm fur coat can provide, secondly to pacify the dog, and thirdly to influence its behaviour. There is no denying the enormous satisfaction that dog lovers get from petting their dogs, but just what effect does our touch have on them?

Ever since human beings started walking on their hind legs they have used their upper limbs to perform numbers of highly intricate and delicate movements. This ability has made them the most complex and destructive animals on earth. Dogs, like their ancestors, have never developed in this way and they use their upper or forelimbs just for basic survival techniques such as running after prey or finding a mate. They do not, for example, point or beckon with their legs, or scratch or caress one another with their paws. Dogs do not congratulate each other by patting each other on the back or shaking paws! The most elaborate responses are those between the mother and her young. Otherwise dogs only use their sense of touch when mouthing in greeting or play, sniffling, bumping one another, or engaging in sexual activity.

Because a dog's body is encased in a permanent cover of hair it presumably makes it less sensitive to pressure or temperature changes.

After years of observing dog behaviour I believe that dogs suffer from pain as we do, and also feel some pleasure in our physical contact with them. However, wolves have never used touch like human beings to show care, attention, and approval to each other and this self-reliant behaviour has been passed on to domestic dogs. All this may explain why dogs can take many knocks and bumps in their stride, and why they wag their tail when patted, but dismiss us quickly for another more meaningful stimulus like food!

TRAINING IMPLICATIONS

Patting and petting dogs as a means of influencing behaviour, e.g. to come when called, is not as effective as we are normally led to believe.

The sense of taste

A dog's sense of taste is not utilised until it has been stimulated by another sense such as smell, hearing or sight. For example, a wolf hears a sound, looks up to investigate it, and sees a small animal running along the ground. He chases and captures the animal using his senses of sight, hearing, touch and smell and then eats his prey. His sense of taste is the last sense to be stimulated.

TRAINING IMPLICATIONS

1. Taste alone cannot be utilised to influence a dog's behaviour during training.
2. Dogs, like humans, develop preferences for certain foods.
3. When offering food as a form of reward we should use the dogs' favourite type. Meat, for a carnivore, would seem the obvious choice.

CHAPTER 2 THE FORMATION OF HABITS OR CONDITIONING

The ideas behind 'conditioning' are based on psychology, a science which explains human and animal behaviour and how the mind works. About a hundred years ago scientists were starting to use psychology to explain the behaviour of human beings, but it has taken a long time for it to be used in a practical way for the training of animals. My method of training dogs is based on a knowledge of psychology and reading this chapter will help you understand why it is so effective. You may think that you are about to embark on some heavy reading and you may feel tempted to skip a few chapters and start training straight away. If you do this, I suggest that you teach one or two exercises at the most so that you can prove to yourself that my method really works. I do hope that you will then return to this chapter as the information in it is the very crux or 'nitty gritty' of my method of training.

Classical conditioning

A Russian physiologist called Ivan Pavlov did a famous experiment on dogs which illustrated a simple process which is now called classical conditioning. He discovered this process almost by accident when he was studying digestion and the way in which saliva is made. Pavlov already knew that dogs salivated when they were given food. Then he realised that the sound of food being prepared also made the dogs salivate.

Next, he tried introducing other stimuli such as ringing a bell before he gave the dogs food. To his amazement, he found that the dogs actually learned to salivate at the sound of a bell which had previously caused no salivation response. Pavlov called this response a conditioned reflex, or conditioned response.

Operant conditioning

Other notable psychologists and behaviourists followed Ivan Pavlov. Thorndike, Watson and Hull to name but a few, made discoveries which helped to explain the learning process.

Then in the 1930s, an American scientist, B. F. Skinner, conducted some experiments which are still having an important effect on psychology.

Skinner developed an experiment to help him understand the way in which behaviour is learned, remembered and forgotten. He placed a rat in a small cage equipped with a lever attached to a food dispenser. Every time the rat pressed the lever, a pellet of food was released into the cage, and this action was timed and mechanically recorded.

Skinner wanted to find out:

(1) Whether the rat would learn to press the lever if food was never made available.

(2) How long it would take for the rat to learn that if it pressed the lever it would get food.

(3) After the rat had learnt to press the lever to obtain food, what would happen if food was given intermittently, or not at all.

As a result of his ingenious experiments Skinner concluded that:

(1) A behaviour or habit will not be learnt if a response is never reinforced, that is, if it never benefits the animal.

(2) A behaviour will rapidly become conditioned (become a habit) if reinforced.

(3) A behaviour which has been learnt will be retained most efficiently if it is reinforced (rewarded) occasionally, rather than every time.

(4) A behaviour which has been learnt will

quickly become 'unlearnt' if the reward is discontinued.

These results help explain human behaviour when gambling. When the response to putting money in the gambling machine is occasionally reinforced with a win, the chances are that the gambler will keep feeding money into the machine in order to gain more and more reinforcement in the shape of money. If the gambler never wins, he will eventually give up and stop responding. Unfortunately, gambling machines are usually geared to offer enough reinforcement to keep us gambling!

There will be a similar reaction when we teach a completely untrained dog to come when called. If its response to come to us is intermittently reinforced, this behaviour will be sustained. If we teach it to come to us and then stop reinforcing the dog completely the habit of coming to us will cease. Without any reinforcement, the habit to come to us will not be established in the first place.

The most important discovery in Skinner's experiments was the power exerted by reinforcement.

Reinforcement

A reinforcement is something which will create or continue a habit. It consists of anything which benefits the animal. There are two main kinds of reinforcers, positive and negative.

POSITIVE REINFORCERS

Positive reinforcers are divided into two classes called primary and secondary.

Primary reinforcers are the most powerful as they consist of things which are essential to survival, such as food or water.

Secondary reinforcers, which are unrelated to survival, can be used with the primary ones at first and will later become reinforcers themselves because they have been linked with the primary ones.

For example, if we call a dog to us and reinforce it with a piece of food when it reaches us, and at the same time say 'Good boy', after a few times, the 'Good boy' alone will become reinforcing to the dog.

Secondary reinforcers have considerably *less* impact or *lasting effect* compared with primary reinforcers. Primary reinforcers must be used with the secondary ones occasionally to keep up their effect.

Patting and petting are often used as reinforcers to try to influence a dog's response. When dog owners come to me for training lessons they often say, 'I pat my dog, but he won't come to me'. The reason is that dogs do not find the effect of being touched very important or beneficial (see chapter 1). I prove this by an experiment which illustrates the effect of different types of reinforcement. A dog is placed between two handlers. They call it in turn and the first handler offers food, while the second gives pats. The dog quickly learns to respond to the food giver and ignore the patter. Food is a primary reinforcer necessary for survival, patting and petting are not. This, of course,

only applies to dogs who have a normal healthy attitude towards food, who 'wolf' their food down. Dogs who are picky or indifferent towards their meals may either have a physical defect, or have been inappropriately fed over a period of time. Leaving food around on tap or offering it too frequently, will often develop an abnormal attitude to food.

Advantages of Positive Reinforcement

1. A dog's instinct will make it use its senses of sight, hearing and smell to investigate its environment and to find food, water and a mate. If we use positive reinforcement when teaching the dog we will be following the same natural process. This is explained fully in chapter 4.
2. The dog *chooses* to respond to your signals because it enjoys the food given as a positive reinforcement.
3. It develops an excellent relationship with its handler because it is never forced to respond against its will.
4. The dog develops a bold, outgoing attitude because it never learns to fear the handler or its environment.
5. The dog is very eager to learn because of the positive reinforcements and because the handler never has to pressurise it or punish it.
6. Many lessons can be learnt when the puppy is very young and in a short time. For example, by eight weeks of age a puppy can learn to sit, stand and drop, stay, come when called, and heel beside you

off the lead. This may sound impossible, but I can assure you, it is true!

7. The behaviour learnt by this method will last for life provided that it is reinforced occasionally.

Disadvantages of Positive Reinforcement

1. A number of repetitions of the behaviour must occur before conditioning takes place. Most dogs will learn with four to six repetitions, some may take as many as a dozen.

2. The dog must have a normal healthy appetite and be motivated by food, therefore training should take place before feeding rather than after!

NOTE: It is extremely difficult to train a dog which is very frightened. Fear will override all other responses. Fear may be exhibited by dogs who have been inadequately socialised (see chapter 3) or who have been exposed to harsh treatment. I have had great success in overcoming this problem with specialised training techniques.

PUNISHMENT AND NEGATIVE REINFORCEMENT

Negative reinforcement is completely different, although it can also be used to teach behaviour. The main disadvantage of using negative reinforcement is that one must precede the reinforcement with either a punishment, or the threat of punishment.

A punishment is an aversive event which an animal – or human – obviously wishes to avoid because of its painful or fearful consequences. A punishment is designed to make a behaviour less likely to occur in the future, e.g. a jerk on the neck with a choker chain will stop a dog surging in front of the handler. If the dog then heels beside the handler's left leg, the chain goes slack. The stopping of the pain and pressure on the dog's neck is a *negative reinforcement* to the dog. It is reinforcing because it *removes* something which is not of benefit to the dog.

'Why shouldn't we use negative reinforcement as well as positive reinforcement when training our dogs?' There is no doubt that an animal will learn if we use punishment and negative reinforcement as a means of training as all reinforcers, whether positive or negative, make a behaviour more likely to occur in the future. However, punishment and negative reinforcement produce involuntary behaviour, as the dog doesn't willingly do what you want. Just imagine how you would feel if a powerful person punished you for a particular action and you didn't understand why. You would probably run away from that situation and avoid contact with that person at all costs in the future. If you were forced to have contact with that person again, you would probably experience the typical signs and symptoms of fear and anxiety.

This is exactly what happens to a dog following punishment. He cannot escape because he has a chain around his neck attached to a lead which prevents him from moving away, so he reacts instead by becoming unwilling and fearful.

Advantages

A severe punishment may have a long-lasting impact on the behaviour of the dog, so much so, that he may never repeat the behaviour that caused the punishment. However, most sensitive dog lovers would not choose to inflict punishment of this severity.

Disadvantages

1. The dog doesn't willingly do what you want.
2. Moderate punishment followed by negative reinforcement will teach the dog after a *considerable* number of repetitions. However, the punishment will have to become progressively more severe if the dog is to continue to obey you.
3. The dog will link its handler with the punishment, and this may destroy the relationship between the dog and the handler.
4. Because the dog responds through fear it may become unwilling, or unable, to learn.
   These disadvantages often result in:
   (a) The dog heeling with tail held low and ears laid back.
   (b) Obvious reluctance to return to the handler on the 'recall', i.e. the dog returns slowly in an arc, rather than quickly in a straight line.
   (c) Cringing behaviour when close to the handler.
   (d) Sycophantic behaviour at the end of training probably intended to ingratiate the dog with the handler.

When I studied the information available on the effects of positive reinforcement, and alternatively punishment and negative reinforcement, it seemed very clear to me which theory I should employ when training dogs. The method I developed using positive reinforcement will be explained in chapter 5.

Chapter 3 will deal with the effects that the environment and early experience has on the development of good temperament and the puppy's ability to learn.

Rain stops play.

CHAPTER 3 SOCIALISATION

Although socialisation is not strictly speaking something which you need to teach your dog, it *is* something which your dog will teach itself provided you give it the opportunity to do so, but *only* if you give it that opportunity. It is so important for your dog's happiness and makes the training of your dog so much easier that I have written a whole chapter about it.

Two dictionary definitions of socialisation are 'make fit for life in companionship with others' and, 'modifying of behaviour especially that of the growing young'. Socialisation is as important for a puppy as a child. Every year many thousands of dogs are destroyed because they develop bad habits which their owners can't control. A lot of these problems are caused by the lack of socialisation of young puppies. Owners often notice temperament problems such as fear or aggression, but they don't bother to do anything about them because it is assumed that the puppy will grow out of them. In most cases, they grow into them! Behavioural problems such as digging holes, excessive barking and pulling washing off the line can also get worse as the dog gets older, often at sexual maturity. I frequently get phone calls with the caller announcing 'I have a problem with my dog, it's seven months old'.

This lack of socialisation in dogs is a fairly recent problem. Until 12,000 years ago, when man started to intervene in the wolf's social structure, dogs would have been socialised within the pack. In our modern society, people usually own one or two dogs at most. As a result, puppies are often isolated from other dogs at a very young age, usually at about eight weeks old when they are taken to their new home.

It is often said that their human family becomes their pack, but this does not take into consideration their need to mix with their own kind. Dogs brought up in a human environment often relate very well to human beings but have not been given the opportunity to learn canine social skills. In order to do this we must try to give our puppies the chance to mix with other dogs as they would in a pack. This may be difficult to organise, but every effort should be made to provide a suitable environment so that when they grow up they can meet strange dogs without fighting, running away, or displaying other anti-social behaviour.

The socialisation of dogs is such a new idea that it is difficult to persuade dog owners that it is necessary. This is made even more difficult by the conflicting advice often given by veterinarians. Professors John Scott and John Fuller, two well-known psychologists, have studied the behavioural development of dogs from birth to adulthood over twenty years. They discovered that the most important period for socialising dogs, is between three and twelve weeks of age. As most people get a puppy when it is eight weeks old, this means that there is only another four weeks of this important period left.

Canine behaviourists such as myself help with problems relating to a dog's psychological well-being. Veterinarians mainly look after their physical well-being. Naturally, advising owners about the potential health risks from such diseases as Distemper, Hepatitis and Parvo Virus is part of their training and, as a result, they usually advise owners to keep puppies at home until four months of age when their immunisation programme is complete. So there is a conflict of interests between canine behaviourists and veterinarians, with the former saying 'Take your dog out and about', and the latter saying 'Keep your dog isolated at home'. Socialisation is as important as a dog's physical health because non-socialisation invariably leads to behavioural or temperament problems. The only solution is for veterinarians and canine behaviourists to get together to discuss this important issue for the sake of both dogs and their owners.

What difference does it make whether we socialise a dog or not? Professors Scott and Fuller found that puppies deprived of human contact until seven weeks of age took two days to make even the slightest contact. Those deprived until fourteen weeks behaved like wild dogs, exhibiting a great fear of human beings. Puppies who have not been given the opportunity to meet other dogs and people outside the immediate family during this period are more likely to be frightened of other dogs, unfamiliar people, and changes in environment.

It is a sobering thought that over 50,000 healthy dogs are destroyed each year in Victoria, Australia, mainly as a result of behavioural problems related to lack of socialisation and attention. This completely overshadows the death rate from all the known infectious diseases. The 'social rejection' disease is in epidemic proportions. The cure is common sense.

In order to help owners overcome this problem and socialise their puppies, I started a club based on my method of training which restricted entry to puppies between eight and sixteen weeks old. The club was named 'The Kintala Club', Kintala being an aboriginal word for dog. Eligible puppies and their owners meet once a week in a park to allow the puppies to play and socialise freely without the restraint of leads. Each week after play they receive basic training using the M.I.D.I. method (see chapter 5). After completing a four-week course they graduate to the adult dog classes where unrestricted socialisation continues before and after training.

The Kintala Club has now been operating for fourteen years and the results have been outstanding. The dogs trained in this system can be described as bold and friendly to both humans and dogs and the club and my training establishment have proved that puppies can have the best of both worlds by getting regular immunisation and veterinary care, combined with early socialisation and training with other immunised dogs and puppies. To date, only one club dog has ever contracted an infectious disease (Parvo Virus) and I do not believe that this was the result of club activities. This dog recovered and no other dog showed any symptoms of the disease.

I strongly believe that all prospective puppy owners should be advised to socialise their puppies as well as follow a programme of immunisation. Many breeders and veterinarians need to change their attitudes and encourage appropriate socialisation and thus the development of temperamentally sound animals. Sometimes good socialisation is provided at a very early age almost by accident. Some small breeders allow their puppies to be born and raised inside the home. This permits constant interaction between the puppies, members of the family and, later, prospective owners. On the negative side, these pups may have little contact with the outside world. On the other hand, some breeding kennels are well away from the house allowing for only occasional contact with the breeders and visitors.

Then comes the time for the puppy to go to its new home. The new owner may be away all day leaving the puppy in an isolated and unchanging environment. Some owners think that because they have a large garden or an older dog for the puppy to play with, the puppy will become socialised as a matter of course. Unfortunately this does not happen. So, how should we socialise our puppies successfully?

First of all make sure that the puppy has commenced its immunisation programme. Then make every effort to take it out to meet other healthy immunised puppies on a regular basis. Expose it to all kinds of different environments and situations. For instance, visit different parks, go to the beach, watch a train go past and ride in the car. Let your pup go into the water with another dog who loves swimming. In short, take it everywhere you go, particularly during that critical time between eight and twelve weeks. You will be rewarded by having a dog which can cope with almost any situation, who loves being with you but who is not overly excited or nervous about change – and one that is easy to train!

The next chapter is about house training your puppy. If your dog is already house trained you can go on to chapter 5.

CHAPTER 4 HOUSE TRAINING

Often the first question I am asked when clients bring a young puppy for training is 'What is the secret of successful house training?' They have tried smacking the pup when it wets in the house, rubbing its nose in its droppings, giving it a dirt box and putting paper down on the laundry floor, all to no avail. There are no magic remedies, but there *is* a simple and effective teaching process which will bring about speedy results.

The need to urinate or defecate is as natural a function for dogs as it is for humans. It takes a long time to toilet train a baby, yet puppies are expected to know what to do almost instantly! At eight weeks old a puppy has little bladder or bowel control, but it will develop them rapidly over the next couple of months. To teach or condition a puppy to eliminate (pooh and wee) in a certain spot we need to know two things, that is, the natural eliminative behaviour of wolves and dogs and how puppies learn.

It is natural for a female wolf or dog to lick her puppies to stimulate urination and defecation. She cleans up the deposits by eating them, and this keeps the den or sleeping area clean. As soon as the pups start crawling around at three to four weeks old they will instinctively try to leave their sleeping area to urinate and defecate. It is important that we remember this fact when house training.

We also need to remember how puppies learn (chapter 2). For example, if we reinforce or reward a response such as urinating outside with something which is important to the puppy such as a piece of food, then the puppy will tend to respond by urinating outside again when it is stimulated by a full bladder.

House training should start the moment you arrive home with your puppy so that you avoid having any 'accidents' right from the beginning. I suggest that you start before you even enter the house by taking the puppy to the area you want it to use. Let it explore the area and if it obliges by urinating or defecating, praise it and give it a small piece of food. Incidentally the spot that you choose for the toilet area should not be too far from the house as you won't want to walk too far on cold wet nights!

Now take your pup inside and follow these instructions:

1. Set your watch or alarm clock to ring in one hour. When this time is up, walk your puppy outside to 'the spot' and stay there for five minutes or so. If it 'wees' or 'poohs', praise it and give it a small piece of food, then take it inside and set your alarm for another hour, and so on. If your puppy does not oblige during the five minute period, take it inside but go out ten minutes later and keep doing this until your patience is rewarded. You will quickly work out your little puppy's own rhythm.

2. Also take the puppy out as soon as it wakens from sleep, after eating or drinking and when it has been chewing on a toy or after prolonged play.

3. Watch its body language carefully for any signs which may indicate a need to go out. Circling and sniffing are often signs it wants to go to the toilet.

4. When you are not able to watch your puppy for a while, either leave it in a secure part of the garden or confine it to a small area in the house such as a baby's playpen. The playpen should contain the puppy's bed and a non-spill bowl of water. A playpen has the distinct advantage of being portable so you can move it from room to room and keep half an eye on the puppy. You will recall that a pup has a natural tendency not to soil its sleeping area, so it will tend to move around or whine in the playpen when it wants to go out which should give you ample opportunity to walk it outside to your selected toilet area.

You have probably gathered by now that what you are doing is anticipating the puppy's behaviour (elimination) so that you can produce the response you want (the pup eliminating in the garden) which in turn is reinforcing or beneficial to the puppy especially if you offer a piece of food straight after the act.

Night time house training

A pup's bladder is not mature enough to go through the night without emptying. You can deal with this by taking your pup out just before you go to bed and then confining it to the playpen which you can place close to your bed. Attach a small bell to your pup's collar so that the tinkle wakens you when the puppy becomes restless. If you are a heavy sleeper you will need to set your alarm and take the puppy out a maximum of five to six hours later. Protect your carpet in case of accidents!

There are some people who prefer to leave their pup outside or in the laundry at night. I don't recommend that you do either, as both will make the pup stressed by being alone. Remember that you have taken it away from its litter so it is your responsibility to give the puppy your companionship instead.

Leaving the puppy in the laundry is also counter productive to your house training programme as the pup will be forced to urinate in the house. Whether you put paper down on the floor or not is immaterial, you have still caused the pup to wet in the house. If you are prepared to get up once or twice during the night to take the pup out, this will help, but it will not solve the stress of social isolation.

Accidents in the house

Inevitably one or two accidents will happen, nobody is perfect! It is extremely important never to punish your puppy for eliminating in the house because the pup will associate the punishment with 'the act' rather than its location. In other words it will be frightened to pooh or wee in front of you and will try to hide next time it needs to eliminate. This will be most distressing for the puppy and will cause *major* house training problems.

When accidents happen you should clean the area thoroughly and then deodorise it so that there is no smell of urine left, otherwise the puppy will tend to go back and use that spot again. Don't use ammonia-based cleaning products which will smell like urine to the dog!

The cardinal rules of house training are patience, observation, and the application of appropriate knowledge so that you can produce, and reinforce, the behaviour you want.

REMEMBER

1. Take your puppy out frequently while it is awake, and immediately after eating or sleeping.
2. Let it walk to the door to establish the pattern of going to the door when it needs to go out.
3. Reinforce your puppy with praise and a piece of food when it urinates or defecates outside.
4. Never punish your puppy if it makes a 'mistake'. Clean the area thoroughly and be more observant next time!

If you follow this advice, your puppy should be house trained within two weeks. A marvellous feat considering it may take a human years!

CHAPTER 5 PREPARATION FOR TRAINING

We have almost reached a stage when training can commence. Before we start, we should recap on the way in which dogs learn.

Firstly, the senses must be employed correctly, usually in this order: sight, hearing, smell. Our visual hand signals must be clear, directive, animated and mean something to the dog. They should be made at a time when it can be guaranteed that they will produce the desired response, not when the dog's attention is elsewhere! In the beginning the voice signal should be given immediately after the visual signal, in order to associate it closely with the dog's response. It should be distinct but not loud and demanding. Later, the voice signal can be given simultaneously with the visual signal, when the dog's response is predictable.

Food should be used as a reinforcement instead of any other type of reinforcement because it is natural and most effective.

Positive reinforcement should be employed so the dog makes voluntary, willing responses.

These are the essential ingredients of my method of training which I call the 'M.I.D.I.' method. Midi stands for 'Motivation by the Incentive of Delayed Inducement'. When using my method there is no need for any form of punishment. Words such as 'no', or 'bad dog' or similar expressions will not be necessary, nor will threatening or harassing gestures.

Dogs can only respond voluntarily if they are free of any kind of restraint. With the M.I.D.I. method, there is no physical handling of the dog and movements are not restricted by the use of a lead. A dog can only be trained like this if the method really works. If you follow my instructions you will be able to produce the responses you want speedily and efficiently, in other words, this book will teach you to become an effective dog trainer.

First of all you must choose a place where you can teach your dog which is free of unnecessary distractions such as other dogs or active children. Probably a small area in your house would be best, especially when teaching the first exercises.

Secondly, all training should take place when your dog is keen for food, preferably just before a meal time. In order to build up an appetite it may be necessary to delay the feeding time for several hours depending on the age of the dog. I often tell the owners of adult dogs who are not interested in food, not to feed their dog the night before training. By the following morning they are much more motivated towards food. After two or three similar fasts the dog develops healthy eating habits.

Young puppies under the age of sixteen weeks are usually fed two or three times a day. If you feed a normal meal at breakfast time but delay the midday meal to late afternoon, you will be able to have a training session before that meal. The puppy's third meal can be given later on if it needs it. It is very much a matter of common sense. If your dog is keen to take food from your hand then its eagerness and receptiveness towards you will be self-evident.

The food you select as a reinforcement should be your dog's favourite food. Most healthy dogs prefer meat. Why shouldn't they? They are carnivores after all. There is no reason to cook meat for healthy dogs, provided it has been passed as fit for human consumption. Avoid using food that crumbles. Pieces of biscuit will often fall from your hand or the dog's mouth encouraging it to perpetually search the ground. Even chicken, one of the dog's favourite foods, can offer problems in this regard. Don't give your dog large pieces of food thinking that it will encourage better responses. I have found that 25 mm cubes (1 in.) of meat are most suitable for large breeds, half that size for medium size dogs and sliver sized pieces for small toy dogs. Dry food has two distinct disadvantages, firstly, dogs are inclined to choke on small pieces, and secondly, they need to visit the water bowl frequently. Your training sessions should not be judged by the amount of time spent, but rather by the number of successful responses achieved, and their subsequent reinforcement with food. Approximately 20 to 30 suitable pieces of food will be quite sufficient to reinforce the teaching process in any session. You can keep the meat in a plastic bag in your pocket until you are ready to use it.

People are often advised not to attempt to train a puppy until it reaches five or six months of age, but you will probably be teaching the most difficult exercise of all when your puppy is just eight weeks old, namely house training (see chapter 4). For this, a puppy must learn to indicate its needs by standing near a door at the appropriate time, and whimper or bark to arouse attention. Teaching a puppy to sit, stand or drop is 'a breeze' in comparison.

Most people get a puppy between the ages of eight and ten weeks and this is the time to start training. Puppies younger than eight weeks can be a problem. Their eyesight is not as efficient as an adult dog's so they may have some difficulty in observing visual (hand) signals. On the other hand, a puppy over ten weeks has already developed some habits which will influence its future behaviour, so you must start at once to develop the habits *you want* with early training. In this way your puppy will grow into a dog with the character and temperament of your choice.

Adult dogs have developed countless habits, some good, some bad, and these may temporarily interfere with the new responses you are trying to generate in your training. However, you can easily correct any bad habits by persuading your dog to behave in a way which is inconsistent with its original undesirable behaviour. For example, if your dog jumps up on your clothes, you can change this by signalling it to sit before it has a chance to jump up, and then reinforcing it in that position. Your dog will quickly realise that it is of greater benefit to sit than to jump all over you. If you repeat this a few times the dog will soon establish a new habit. There is absolutely no truth in the old adage 'You can't teach an old dog new tricks.'

Teaching procedure

There is one other piece of important information which I must tell you before we start teaching specific exercises.

A stimulus is something that the dog will respond to. But why should the stimulus of a hand movement and voice signal persuade an untrained dog to adopt positions such as the 'sit', 'stand' or 'drop'. Probably on its own, it won't. However, if you hold food in your hand as an extra stimulus to motivate the dog then you are much more likely to succeed. When *teaching* every exercise, you will use food in your hand as a major inducement to produce the response you want during initial conditioning. You may think the food as a stimulus has to be used constantly rather like the proverbial carrot to the donkey, but it is most important to understand that it is only needed *at first* to shape the desired behaviour.

Once the behaviour has been learnt and the dog is conditioned to perform the action every time, food as a stimulus *must* be eliminated, usually after six to twelve repetitions of the correct response. By this stage, your hand and voice signals alone will produce the appropriate response, in the same way as Pavlov's dogs learnt to respond to the stimulus of a bell even when it was not paired with food.

It is also very important to realise that although food is given every time the dog performs the exercise correctly as a reinforcement during initial conditioning, it must be given only intermittently when practising the exercise once it has been learnt. Remember the gambling machine!

Older dogs, or those with difficult temperaments who have established firm habits will naturally take a little longer to condition, but the procedure is exactly the same.

As you can see this method of training follows a distinct pattern which will become obvious as you work through this book.

Exercises

Glossary

In this book some words are used with special meanings. You will find a full explanation of these words in chapter 2, but I have included a short reminder here for quick reference.

behaviour: the response to a stimulus. For example, when the dog comes to you when you call 'come' and put your hand low to the ground.

condition/conditioned/conditioning: the method by which you can train your dog so the actions you teach it become a habit.

food inducement: a term used to describe food used as a *stimulus* in conjunction with voice and hand signals to shape the behaviour you want when teaching new exercises.

intermittent reinforcement: a reinforcement which is given to the dog at irregular intervals so that the dog cannot predict when it is going to be offered.

offer/offered: in this book 'offer' often means to give a hand or voice signal or to give food.

reinforce/reinforcer/reinforcement: a reinforcement is something which the dog likes and which is given *after* a correct response to a signal to make the dog want to respond to that signal again in the same way. In this book 'reinforce' usually means giving your dog a piece of food such as fresh meat.

respond/response: a response is what the dog does when you have stimulated it. For example, sit, stand, drop.

stimulus/stimulate: a stimulus is anything which will produce a response in your dog. For example, hand or voice signals.

TRAINING CHECK LIST

Please ask yourself the following questions before starting any training session.

1. Is my dog eager for food?
2. Am I using the right kind of food?
3. Are my surroundings suitable for this particular exercise?
4. Am I free of unwanted distractions?
5. Are my clothes suitable for training, i.e. no billowing coats or dresses, no large hats, no heavy boots or flapping footwear.
6. Have I organised any necessary equipment?
7. Have I learnt the appropriate actions for this exercise?

8. Do I understand the M.I.D.I. method? That is:

INITIAL CONDITIONING

(a) I must stimulate the dog to do the exercise by using a hand and voice signal, plus food in the hand as an inducement.

(b) I must generate the correct response.

(c) I must reinforce the correct action instantly after *every* response.

MAINTAINING CONDITIONING

(a) I must stimulate the dog using a hand and voice signal *only*.

(b) I must generate the correct response.

(c) I must reinforce the correct response *intermittently*.

9. If at any time the dog does not respond correctly to my signals, I must go back to the beginning and start teaching the exercise again. I must examine my actions and modify my signals to produce the response I want. I must never blame or punish the dog.

10. Have I practised my actions to get my timing correct? Will my hand actions flow the dog smoothly into the desired position?

NOTE: The hand and voice signals summarised at the end of each exercise are the ones used after the exercise has been taught and the dog is conditioned. Usually these are modified versions of the signals used in initial conditioning, but occasionally the voice and/or hand signal is phased out completely, for example, in the right about turn (exercise 7).

aytime, dingo-style.

EXERCISE 1 THE RECALL

The dog comes when called.

VALUE OF THE RECALL

The recall is probably the most important exercise that you will ever teach your dog. It will allow you to let your dog off the lead in the knowledge that you can call it back when required. Because of this:

1. Your dog will be able to run free of restraint which will exercise it more efficiently, and increase its enjoyment and fitness.

2. The person who exercises the dog will not be constantly pulled along at the end of a lead!

3. The dog can be called away from dangerous situations or when it might frighten other people or animals.

4. Dogs can greet each other naturally when off the lead. They are therefore much less likely to be trig-gered into an act of aggression with another dog and will instead become socially well-behaved creatures (see chapter 3). Unfortunately some dogs are never exercised because their owners are so worried by their dog's anti-social behaviour.

5. You will be able to take the dog into different environments whenever you wish.

6. You will be able to teach your dog other exercises.

All these points can be summarised into one statement.

The 'recall' exercises control over the dog which gives you, the handler, confidence in your own ability.

Prepare yourself and your dog for training as discussed in Chapter 5 and read the check list.

INITIAL CONDITIONING

1. Wait until your dog is looking at you from a short distance away.

2. Move away from your dog to encourage it to come towards you, and drop your hand low to the ground. At this stage your hand should have food in it. You can use either your right or left hand, whichever is more comfortable, but usually the right hand is used.

3. Say, 'come', once only when your dog is actually moving towards you.

4. Reinforce your dog with the piece of food in your hand the moment it reaches you.

5. Remove your hand quickly away up to your waist level.

6. Repeat points 1–5 until the dog's behaviour becomes predictable, i.e. conditioned. This should not take more than a dozen repetitions.

MAINTAINING CONDITIONING

Once the dog's behaviour is predictable and it always comes to you on signal you should do the following to maintain its response:

1. Stop using food in the hand to help to stimulate a response.

2. The hand signal must remain the same whether there is food in the hand or not. Dogs can detect very subtle variations in hand signals.

3. It shouldn't be necessary to move away from your dog unless it is responding slowly.

4. The food which you are going to use as a reinforcer should be kept in a pocket or pouch where the dog cannot see it.

5. It is essential that you stop reinforcing your dog every time it responds correctly, however, do not make the intervals between reinforcers (the food) too long to begin with, e.g. reinforce the second, fifth, first, fourth or sixth response, choosing the quickest responses to reinforce.

Please remember that your reinforcement must become unpredictable so the dog does not know when it will be fed, as discussed in chapter 2.

The difference between initial conditioning and maintaining conditioning should now be clear.

INITIAL CONDITIONING	MAINTAINING CONDITIONING

The Stimulus

(a) Your movement away from the dog.

(b) Your hand signal low to the ground.

(c) Your verbal signal 'come'.

(d) The food in your hand.

(a) Your hand signal low to the ground.

(b) Your verbal signal 'come'.

NOTE: No food to induce the response.

The Response

The dog is *induced* to come in response to the above stimuli.

The dog *comes* in response to the above stimuli.

The Reinforcement

The food given to the dog from your *hand*.

The food given to the dog **INTERMITTENTLY** from your *pocket*.

COMMON HANDLING PROBLEMS

Problem
The dog does not come when called.

Remedy
 1. Make sure that your dog is looking at you before offering signals.
 2. Ensure that your first signal produces the desired response, i.e. *do not* say 'come', more than once. The best way of doing this is to make sure that the dog is only a few paces from you when you say 'come' (see Initial Conditioning, 3) so it does not have time to be distracted before it reaches you. Increase the distance gradually.
 3. Reinforce immediately the dog responds by coming to you.

THE RECALL

Hand signal: Drop your hand low to the ground.
Voice signal: Come.

'Sit!'

EXERCISE 2 THE SIT

The dog sits in front of you following a recall.

The dog sits at your left-hand side.

VALUE OF THE SIT

1. It allows you to put a collar or lead on your dog while the dog is in an accessible, static position.

2. It makes physical examination of the dog easy, particularly of the eyes, ears and mouth.

3. It is a relaxed position for the dog to assume.

4. Small children and elderly people can make friends with the dog easily without fear of being knocked over.

5. The sit exercise can be used with most of the other control exercises and is a prelude to some of them, especially during initial conditioning, e.g. the drop is taught from the sit position.

Sit in Front

INITIAL CONDITIONING

The sit exercise can be combined with the recall exercise in the following way.

1. Call your dog. As it comes close to you, place your right hand, containing food, in front of the dog's nose.

2. Draw this hand in a flowing motion towards your legs and then up to approximately waist height, bringing your body upright at the same time. This will cause the dog to look up and fall into the sit position.

3. Say 'sit' once only, as soon as the dog starts to adopt the sit position.

4. Reinforce the dog with food from your hand the moment its bottom reaches the ground.

5. Remove your hand quickly back to its original position at waist height.

6. Repeat points 1–5 until the dog's behaviour becomes predictable.

The Stimulus
(a) Your hand signal moving from nose level to waist height.
(b) The food in your hand.
(c) Your verbal signal 'sit'.

The Response
The dog sits to the above stimuli.

The Reinforcement
The food which is given to the dog from your hand.

COMMON HANDLING PROBLEMS

Problem
The dog sits away from your legs rather than close to them.

Remedy
Avoid leaning forward to induce the sit response. Bring your right hand close to your legs before raising it to waist level.

Problem
The dog follows the hand up to waist level and finishes standing on its hind legs.

Remedy
Do not leave your hand dangling above the dog's nose. Raise your hand more quickly up to *chest* level, straightening your body at the same time.

Sit at Side

INITIAL CONDITIONING

The dog should be taught to sit at the handler's left-hand side after the sit in front has been repeated only a few times, otherwise the dog can become too conditioned to move around to the front position where it has been reinforced before.

1. With your dog in a standing position at your left side, bring your right hand, containing food, to a position in front of the dog's nose.

2. Raise your hand upwards in a flowing motion to approximately waist level *directly* above the dog's head.

3. Say 'sit', as soon as the dog starts to adopt the sit position.

4. Reinforce the dog immediately its bottom touches the ground.

5. Remove your hand quickly up to waist level.

6. Repeat points 1–5 until the dog's behaviour becomes predictable.

The stimulus, response and reinforcement is the same as in the initial conditioning for the sit in front.

MAINTAINING CONDITIONING

Maintain conditioning as described for the recall exercise by eliminating food as a stimulus and reinforcing the dog intermittently with food from your pocket.

Once you have taught the heeling exercise (exercise 6) you can gradually phase out voice and hand signals for sit if you wish, so that the dog sits automatically when you stop moving.

COMMON HANDLING PROBLEMS

Problem
The dog jumps out of the sit position as you reinforce it with food.

Remedy
Move your hand rapidly from your waist to the dog's mouth when reinforcing, thus preventing any forward movement.

THE SIT IN FRONT

Hand signal: Move your right hand from the level of the dog's nose in a flowing movement towards your legs and then up to approximately waist height. Bring your body upright at the same time.
Voice signal: Sit.

THE SIT AT SIDE

Hand signal: Move your right hand from the level of the dog's nose in a flowing movement *directly* above the dog's head to approximately waist height. Bring your body upright at the same time.
Voice signal: Sit.

NOTE: Competitors in obedience trials are not allowed to give the dog a voice or hand signal to sit. The dog must sit automatically when the handler comes to a halt.

EXERCISE 3 THE STAND

The dog stands beside your left leg.

VALUE OF THE STAND

1. It is easy to groom or bath the dog when standing.

2. The dog can be examined by a veterinary surgeon.

3. It is a requirement of obedience trials.

4. The stand position is used during showing.

NOTE: Your control will increase dramatically when your dog will stand and stay (exercise 5).

INITIAL CONDITIONING

An exercise is often taught in conjunction with another one, e.g. the stand is often taught with the sit, or the stay, or combined with heeling. At this stage, I shall explain the way to teach the stand from the sit position.

1. Sit the dog at your left-hand side (see exercise 2).

2. Place your right hand containing food immediately in front of your dog's nose.

3. Take a small step forward with your left leg, simultaneously moving your right hand forward, thereby drawing the dog into a stand position. Say 'stand' the moment the dog starts to adopt the stand position.

4. Feed the dog immediately its nose reaches your hand, then remove the hand promptly.

5. Allow your dog to remain in the stand position for a few seconds before signalling it to change position.

6. Repeat points 1–5 a few times. Do not repeat any sequence too frequently, e.g. sit, stand, sit, stand, otherwise the dog may begin to sit before you ask it to.

MAINTAINING CONDITIONING

1. Eliminate food as a stimulus.

2. Reinforce the stand with food intermittently.

COMMON HANDLING PROBLEMS

Problem
The dog moves across in front of the handler.

Remedy
The left leg must move forward to keep the dog in a straight line, and the hand position must finish beside this leg at the dog's nose level.

You should not reinforce the sit exercise more often than the stand, otherwise the dog may find the sit more reinforcing and sit when you want it to stand!

Problem
The dog sits after it has been reinforced in the stand position.

Remedy
If the dog sees the hand going from its nose directly to waist level, it may interpret this as a sit signal. It is better if you move your hand across the front of your legs at the dog's nose level until it can be brought up to waist level at the right side of your body without the dog seeing it.

THE STAND

Hand signal: Move your right hand forward at the level of the dog's nose taking a short step forward with the left leg at the same time.
Voice signal: Stand.

EXERCISE 4 THE DROP

The dog lies down at your left-hand side.

VALUE OF THE DROP

1. The dog can take up this relaxed position if you want it to be quiet and still in the house.

2. If injuries occur they can be treated easily and the dog can be examined for parasites.

3. The dog may be happy to stay in this position for a long time during stripping, trimming, or grooming.

4. It is an obedience trial requirement.

5. The dog is more likely to stay in a drop position than in a stand or sit position. This is helpful when teaching the 'stay' (exercise 5).

INITIAL CONDITIONING

It is easier to teach the basic drop exercise from the sit position. The dog should lie down looking alert as illustrated in the photograph rather than rolling over on its side.

1. Sit your dog beside your left leg.

2. Quickly bring your right hand, containing food, to a point directly in front of your dog's nose.

3. Take a *short* step forward with your left leg and at the same time move your hand slowly, at first, and obliquely down towards the ground.

4. Turn the palm of your hand down so that the food is between your hand and the ground. Obviously you will have to bend your knees a lot so that you can take up this position.

5. Say 'drop' as soon as your dog starts to extend its legs forward into the drop position.

6. Feed the dog immediately it lies down.

7. Move your hand quickly out of sight keeping it low to the ground until you can bring it up beside the right side of your body without the dog seeing it. Stand upright at the same time.

8. Now bring your dog into a sit position and repeat points 2–7 a few times.

MAINTAINING CONDITIONING

Before attempting to drop your dog without food in your hand, it is best gradually to increase the speed of your hand signal, to that the dog responds more quickly. Once the dog responds quickly you can maintain conditioning in the usual way.

Dropping Your Dog in a Relaxed Position

When you have taught the dog to drop in the way described above, it is easy to change your signals slightly so that the dog ends up in a relaxed position such as lying on its side. Substitute the voice signal 'lie down' for 'drop' and pat the ground a few times to encourage the dog to lie down.

COMMON HANDLING PROBLEMS

Problem
The dog does not adopt the drop position.

Remedy
1. The position of the food in your hand may be incorrect. Look carefully at the photographs.
2. Your hand movement may be too rapid. Draw your dog down nice and slowly.
3. The angle of descent of your hand to the ground may induce the dog to stand instead of drop.

4. Your hand may be too close to the dog's face making it back away.

NOTE: It is sometimes more difficult to get a dog with long limbs to lie down. In this case it may be necessary to reinforce 'successive approximations' to the drop position. For example:

(a) Feed the dog as it begins to lower its head to follow your right hand down towards the ground.
(b) Feed again as the dog lowers its head a little further and puts one leg forward.
(c) Feed again as it puts both legs forward.
(d) Finally reinforce the dog as it goes into the drop position.

THE DROP

Hand signal: Move your right hand obliquely towards the ground, turning the palm of your hand down so it faces the ground.
Voice signal: Drop.

Just good friends.

EXERCISE 5 THE STAY

The dog stays in the same position until otherwise directed.

VALUE OF THE STAY

1. This exercise gives you a great deal of control over the dog's activities. For instance, it can be told to stay while a photograph is being taken, before eating, during a veterinary examination, when grooming, etc. As a result, your dog will be socially acceptable to your vet, friends and family.

2. It is an obedience trial requirement and is used in the show ring.

3. The stay exercise can be useful for reducing activity in an over-active dog.

It is important to remember that you must only use the stay exercise when you genuinely want your dog to stay in one position until you return to it. Your dog will quickly become confused if, for example, you tell it to stay when you leave home to go to work. In this situation you don't really want it to stay in one position until you get home, so you can say something else such as 'goodbye' instead.

When teaching the stay exercise, you must realise that dogs, like humans, become physically tired if they are required to remain in one position for any length of time. Consequently your training should not be prolonged. Changing the dog's position between the sit, stand and drop will help.

INITIAL CONDITIONING

The sit stay

1. Eliminate any distractions, especially moving objects.

2. Place your dog in the sit position at your left-hand side (exercise 2).

3. Say the word 'stay', then step forward one pace with your right leg keeping the left leg static. Do not use a hand signal as this may encourage your dog to move forward.

4. Before the dog attempts to move, step back to your original position and give it a piece of food immediately.

5. Repeat points 3 and 4 a few times.

6. Gradually increase the distance you move away from your dog to two, three, four steps and so on.

7. When you can move about four steps away, turn round and face your dog, then return to it almost immediately. Give it a piece of food.

The drop stay

Follow the same procedure as for the sit stay.

Your dog is more likely to stay in the drop position simply because it is comfortable for it, and because it requires more energy to move from that position. Consequently, it will be easier for you to anticipate any possible movement when the dog is lying down. Often a dog will rest its head on its paws, or roll over on one hip, which will make any potential break from position even more obvious to the handler.

When reinforcing the dog in the drop position, it may be advantageous to place a piece of dry food between the dog's paws. This will take longer to chew and swallow than fresh meat. Looking at it from the dog's point of view, 'Why get up when what I want is down here?'

The stand stay

When teaching the stand stay you need to be very alert. Your dog should not move even one foot. It is so easy for the dog to move from the stand position, that I suggest you stand it on a slight incline to begin with to minimise the possibility of movement. When standing uphill, the hind legs are stretched further back and the forelegs firmly planted because the dog must lean forward to maintain its centre of gravity.

Follow the same teaching procedure as for the sit stay. At first, any movement away from your dog after you have told it to stay should be very small. Don't move your hands around because they will probably be very close to the dog's face and may tempt it to break from position.

MAINTAINING CONDITIONING

Your observation, timing and common sense should ensure good progress. You should never 'test' your dog by trying to advance too quickly. Remember the M.I.D.I. method is based on the principle that you and your dog must be successful at each stage of the exercise before moving on to the next. One extra step at a time in the stay exercise will bring about remarkable results in a very short time. Introduce a visual hand signal as you say 'stay' when you are sure that your dog will not move from its position. It is usual to place your right hand in front of the dog's face.

Reinforce the stay exercise intermittently once your dog has learnt the exercise.

The 'Wait' signal

When teaching the more advanced exercises (e.g. exercises, 12, 17, 18) which require the dog to stay in one position until it is called or sent from that position, it is better to use a different voice signal such as 'wait', together with the usual stay hand signal.

Remember, the voice signal 'stay' must only be used if you want your dog to stay in one position until you return to it.

Problem

The dog breaks from position.

Remedy

1. Remove distractions.

2. Go back to 'initial conditioning' and slowly build up the distance between you and your dog again.

3. Keep your hands absolutely still. Because of the important role your hands play in reinforcing and stimulating your dog, any hand gesture or finger-wagging will encourage your dog to move forward to investigate them. For this reason it is not advisable to use hand signals during early training of the stay exercise.

4. Watch carefully for any indications that your dog is likely to break from the stay position, e.g. ears pricking up, head movements or tail-wagging. Return to your dog immediately.

5. Avoid showing the food until you have returned to your dog's side as this may cause it to break from position.

It can be helpful to practise the stay when your dog is tired after exercise! Always make your surroundings and your dog's condition work to your advantage during training.

Remember that if the dog moves from the stay position it is your fault because you are the teacher and it will delay progress if you blame the dog. For some reason, some people tend to become rather threatening when a dog breaks from a stay position. Growling at the dog will only create fear and unwillingness in it. If you simply go back to the beginning you will quickly become successful.

THE STAY

Hand signal: Place your right hand in front of the dog's face.

Voice signal: Stay.

'Staying' at the Kintala Club.

EXERCISE 6 HEELING

The dog walks or runs beside your left leg, on or off the lead.

VALUE OF HEELING

1. The dog can be taken for a walk without causing an obstruction to either the handler or other people walking in the same area.

2. Owners of dogs who have been taught to heel are more likely to exercise their dogs because they can walk in a controlled and comfortable way. Dogs who pull on the lead are often left at home, which makes any bad habits they may have worse because the dog is bored from lack of exercise and an unchanging environment.

3. It is an obedience trial and show ring requirement.

INITIAL CONDITIONING

This difficult exercise requires excellent timing on the part of the handler. Unlike the previous stationary exercises, your dog will move with you into a constantly changing environment with all its distractions. In order to compete with these distractions you must give clear and meaningful signals and reinforce the dog when it is in the correct position close to your left leg. It may help if you begin to teach this exercise in a long, narrow passageway, using this environment to help you shape the right response. It is important, however, never to crowd the dog when you do this.

1. Start with your dog in the sit or stand position at your left-hand side. Carry several pieces of food in your left hand and a piece in your right hand. Both hands should be held at waist level.

2. Step off with your left leg, simultaneously sweeping your right hand forward parallel to your dog at its eye level.

3. As your dog moves forward say 'heel'.

4. Move your right hand back to waist level as you take three to four brisk paces.

5. After three to four paces, signal your dog to stand as described in exercise 3, and reinforce your dog instantly.

6. Take another piece of food in your right hand and repeat points 2–5 a number of times.

NOTE: It is most important that you reinforce your dog when it is close to your left leg, and not when it is lagging behind you or surging ahead.

MAINTAINING CONDITIONING

This is done in the usual way by eliminating food as a stimulus and gradually increasing the heeling distance literally step by step. It is best if you give short enjoyable lessons measured by the distance covered rather than the amount of time spent in training. Three or four heeling routines, each of twenty to thirty paces, is ample. If you multiply this by three or four training sessions per week you will have walked more than 400 metres in the heeling position. Enough to make Rin Tin Tin look inadequate!

Never go on training if your dog is getting bored. Your dog should look willing and happy during training at all times.

COMMON HANDLING PROBLEMS

Problem
The dog surges in front of the handler.

Remedy
Give the visual heeling signal with your left hand instead of your right. Also give the stand signal and offer the reinforcement with your left hand. This will alter your dog's point of interest to your left side rather than slightly ahead of you.

Problem
The dog lags behind you.

Remedy
There are a number of different reasons for lagging with the remedy being dependent on the cause.

1. Your dog may not be eager for food. Make sure it is prepared for training as discussed in chapter 5.

2. Your hand signal may not be clear or directive enough. Signal with your right hand.

3. Train when your dog is feeling energetic so that you are able to reinforce your dog for a lively heeling action.

NOTE: You may make the dog lag more if you falter or slow down when it falls behind you. You must try to time your actions to produce the desired result every time.

Problem
The dog jumps up and down whilst heeling.

Remedy
1. Make sure that your hand returns to waist level immediately after you have offered the visual heeling signal. Never leave your hand dangling above the dog's face.

2. Take only a few steps and feed your dog before it can jump up. Your timing is critical.

Problem
The dog deviates from your left leg whilst heeling.

Remedy
1. Begin your heeling exercise beside a wall or in a corridor in your house, so that your dog is not physically able to move away from your left leg. Then progress to heeling in a less restricted place or:

2. Quickly make a gesture with your left hand to attract the dog back to you. Maintain your dog's interest by moving quickly and keeping training sessions short.

HEELING

Hand signal: Step off with your left leg, simultaneously sweeping your right hand forward parallel to your dog at its eye level. Move your hand back to waist level as you take a number of brisk paces.
Voice signal: Heel.

Follow the leader at the Kintala Club.

7 TURNING WHILE HEELING

VALUE OF TURNS

1. Turns allow you and your dog to change direction in a controlled manner.

2. They are an obedience trial requirement.

Right about turn

The dog and handler both turn 180 degrees to the right so that they walk back on the same line as they travelled before the turn.

INITIAL CONDITIONING

1. Stand your dog at your left-hand side.

2. Place your right hand, containing food, at a point slightly in front of your right leg, level with your dog's nose.

3. As your dog steps across in front of you to investigate your hand, pivot on the spot, 180 degrees. Your dog will follow your moving hand as you turn provided you do not turn too quickly to begin with.

4. When you have completed the turn, either stand or sit your dog, and reinforce immediately.

5. Repeat points 1–4 several times.

6. Now repeat points 1–4 at a slow pace, and then at a normal pace, taking a few paces after the turn before you reinforce your dog.

MAINTAINING CONDITIONING

Phase out the use of food as a stimulus and allow your hand signal to become systematically less obvious until finally the dog turns with the handler auto-matically. Produce rapid tight turns and reinforce these intermittently.

COMMON HANDLING PROBLEMS

Problem
The dog turns with the handler but does not stay close to the handler's legs.

Causes
1. The handler may be walking in an arc rather than pivoting on the balls of the feet.
2. The handler's right hand may be extended too far from the legs.

3. The hand may not be held low enough.

Remedy
The remedy is obvious and depends on the cause.

Left about turn

The dog turns 180 degrees to the right as before,
while the handler turns 180 degrees to the left.

INITIAL CONDITIONING

This exercise requires a great deal of co-ordination on the part of the handler. I recommend that you practise the movements without your dog a few times before beginning to teach the exercise. At first do the exercise slowly.

1. Stand your dog at your left-hand side.

2. Place your right hand containing food at a point slightly in front of your right leg, level with your dog's nose.

3. As your dog steps across in front of you to investigate your hand, turn *left* 180 degrees. Your dog continues to turn right following your right hand which continues to move behind your back.

4. As you complete the turn of 180 degrees, drop your left hand down and give the hand signal for heel (see exercise 6). Take a few steps, then reinforce immediately with food from the right hand.

5. Repeat points 1–4 several times.

6. Progress so that the exercise is done at a normal pace.

MAINTAINING CONDITIONING

Use the same procedure as in the right about turn.

COMMON HANDLING PROBLEMS

Problem
The dog does not complete the 180 degree turn to the right but cuts back to the wrong side of the handler. The remedy depends on the cause.

Cause
  1. The right hand signal may be given too quickly for the dog to follow.
  2. The handler may be moving off before the dog has committed itself to the turn.

  3. The right hand may be left in a position which stimulates the dog at a time when the left hand should be taking over.

Remedy
Modify your actions according to the cause of the problem.

RIGHT ABOUT TURN

Hand signal: Place your right hand in front of your right leg level with the dog's nose and pivot 180 degrees to the right, gradually phasing out the use of a hand signal.
Voice signal: None.

LEFT ABOUT TURN

Hand signal: Place your right hand in front of your right leg level with the dog's nose and turn *left* 180 degrees as your dog turns right. Drop your left hand down after you have turned and give the hand signal for heel. Gradually phase out the use of hand signals.
Voice signal: None.

EXERCISE 8 <u>HEEL ON LEAD</u>

The dog heels beside the left leg with a lead attached to its collar.

A fairly long lead should be used for reasons which will be explained below. Up to this point, your dog has been taught to heel beside you without any form of restraint. It is particularly important to teach puppies without a lead at first. The restraint imposed by a lead often produces frantic attempts on the part of a puppy to free itself, by tugging, yelping, twisting, biting the lead or even lying flat on the ground in a submissive manner.

Training 'off lead' teaches the dog to enjoy heeling beside you, so that when a lead is put on it acts more as an ornament than anything else.

When starting to train on a lead, it is best if you place the end of a lightweight, 2 metre long lead in

your left-hand pocket allowing a distinct loop to form between you and the dog. Both hands should adopt the off lead position (see exercise 6) and you should practice the exercise as if the lead did not exist. Later the lead can be taken out of your pocket and held in the usual way. The lead should be attached to the dog's everyday fixed collar.

Correction chain collars are unnecessary and in my view indicate that handlers cannot teach exercises without the use of force. Unfortunately, choker chains are often used to punish a dog, frequently in an aggressive manner. This can quickly damage a dog both physically and emotionally. Many owners quite unwittingly teach their dogs to tug and pull. Their dogs literally take *them* for a walk. Very early in life a dog learns that if it pulls its owner to an upright object, such as a tree, or rock, it will gain the benefit of sniffing all the important doggy odours! Conditioning to pull is quickly established.

You can teach or reteach your dog to walk at heel if you use the heeling methods described in exercise 6.

Taking your dog for a walk on a lead

I often see people taking their dog for a walk on a very short tight lead and ask myself 'What enjoyment can there be for the dog?' I have always felt that the main purpose of dog walking is to allow the dog to indulge in all the normal canine activities, and to have fun.

Local Government Rules and Regulations often restrict the freedom of dogs by requiring them to be on a lead, more's the pity. However, this problem can be minimised by making, or purchasing, a lead about four metres long or acquiring one that is retractable.

In a semi-free state the dog can at least engage in much natural behaviour such as sniffing trees, meeting other dogs and people, and of course, defecating and urinating in preferred spots.

Naturally, a long lead needs to be handled sensibly; letting it out and taking up the slack requires a little more attention. The added pleasure it will give your dog makes the extra effort all worthwhile.

Tight leads which create an unnatural amount of restriction often lead to problems such as fear or aggression (see chapter 3).

Left about turn on a lead

This turn, often referred to as the pivot turn, can get an untrained handler into one or two knots! Your actions and those of your dog remain virtually the same as the turn without a lead (exercise 7). The only real difference is that you start with the lead in the left hand and pass it across to your right hand as you turn left. Your right hand goes behind your back and returns the lead to the left hand just as you are completing the turn. Confusing?! If you read through the description slowly and practice the actions without your dog, everything will soon fall into place.

EXERCISE 9 RETURN TO HEEL

The dog moves from a position in front of the handler, to one where it is sitting beside the handler's left leg.

In exercises such as the recall, retrieving and jumping, the dog is expected to return and sit in front of the handler. It is then directed to go around the back of the handler finishing in a sit position at the handler's left-hand side. This is called the 'return to heel'. From this position, both the handler and dog are ready to go on with other exercises.

I prefer to teach dogs to return straight to the heel position without sitting in front first unless the dog is going to compete in obedience or field trials when the sit in front is compulsory for many exercises. After all, when we are walking our dogs and we want them to come to us and be under control, we simply call them to come to the heel position. People don't often practise the rigid obedience routine when walking in the park! The same principle applies to retrieving. It is just as easy to take an article from a dog's mouth when it is beside you as in front of you.

In my opinion the governing bodies of obedience trials should alter the way exercises are scored so that a handler and dog team cannot be failed if they perform the essential part of an exercise satisfactorily but don't fulfill some minor requirement.

For example, at the present time a dog can fail a retrieving exercise simply because it anticipates the return to heel and fails to sit in front, even though it has retrieved and given up the article to the handler. Surely the essence of the exercise has been successfully carried out and the dog should be marked accordingly? Many people think that there are a number of rules and regulations which are too rigid and seem to have been drawn up in the expectation that handlers will act like sergeant-majors. I would like to see more spontaneity and enjoyment in the attitude and performance of many dogs taking part in trials.

INITIAL CONDITIONING

1. Start with your dog sitting in front of you. Hold a piece of food in each hand at waist level.

2. Drop your right hand down slightly to the right of your knee, or lower for small dogs. As the dog moves forward to investigate your hand, take one short step backwards with your right leg, moving the right hand back so that it remains close to your knee. Your right hand should finish slightly beyond the back of your right leg. At this point give the voice signal 'heel'.

3. As your dog follows your right hand, lower your left hand behind your back to stimulate your dog to move towards that hand. As it does so, move your right hand out of reach.

4. Draw your dog forward with your left hand until it is beside your left leg, then give the sit hand signal by raising the left hand (see exercise 2). Simultaneously move your right foot back to its original position.

5. Reinforce the dog, then return your hands to their original position.

Gradually make your hand and leg movements more subtle until a small backward movement of your right hand will produce the required response.

MAINTAINING CONDITIONING

Reinforce the response intermittently.

COMMON HANDLING PROBLEMS

Problem
The dog cuts back to the handler's right side.

Remedy
1. Make your actions slow to begin with so that the dog can easily follow your hands.
2. Make your left hand action more obvious, or lower to the ground.
3. Do not allow the right hand to dangle behind your back so that it attracts the dog away from your left hand.

RETURN TO HEEL

Hand signal: Move your right hand a short distance from in front of your right leg to just behind it like a pendulum.
Voice signal: Heel.

10 FIGURE OF 8, OR, OBSTACLE WEAVING

The dog weaves around obstacles or people in the heeling position.

VALUE OF WEAVING

1. The dog learns to negotiate obstacles keeping close to the handler. This is useful when walking in a crowded environment.

2. The figure of 8 exercise is an obedience trial requirement.

You will require the help of two people as markers or you can use two upright objects placed 3 metres apart. In obedience trials, the judge tells the hand-ler to halt beside one of the people during the figure of 8. The dog must automatically assume the sit position.

This exercise is relatively simple providing you have taught your dog to heel close to your left leg, but there are a couple of potential problems related to the angle of approach to the markers. The photographs illustrate the correct and incorrect way.

CORRECT

In this photograph the handler goes close to the red marker, but approaches the yellow marker in a wide circle in order to allow sufficient room for the dog to negotiate the object. This also produces quicker, smoother heeling.

INCORRECT

In this photograph the handler's path from the red marker to the yellow marker does not give the dog enough room to negotiate the object. As a result it is likely to walk around the wrong side of the yellow marker. Obviously the cramped circling will also affect the smoothness of the heeling performance.

Bliss!

EXERCISE 11 THE SHOW DOG, INCLUDING STAND FOR EXAMINATION

The demands of the show ring are fairly simple. The dog is required to heel beside the handler on the lead and to stand still while it is examined, either on the ground or on a table, depending on the breed of dog. However, the dog often has to endure prolonged grooming periods, long hours of travelling, and many hours of waiting either near the show ring or confined in a dog trailer. Sometimes the dog is also required to adopt exaggerated postures called 'stacking' to show off its best features. All this may stress the dog and lead to many of the behavioural problems which I see frequently in my practice. These include:

1. Cringing away from the judge (the most common problem).
2. Biting the judge.
3. Fear of the judging table.
4. Nervous behaviour in the ring.
5. Dull, unhappy performances.
6. Fear of other dogs in the ring.
7. Attacking other dogs.
8. Boisterous, uncontrolled behaviour.

Let us look at some ways of avoiding or curing the problems listed above.

Problems 1-5

These problems indicate that the dog is not enjoying the show ring environment.

Remedy
First of all, teach the stand for examination using the M.I.D.I. method of training so that your dog enjoys being touched and finds it a rewarding experience.

If your dog is excessively nervous you will have to do some preparation before you teach the formal stand for examination exercise. I suggest that you first teach your dog to enjoy approaching humans. You can do this by getting friends to walk away from the dog with their backs to it with food in their hands. They should drop their hands down low as they walk, to encourage the dog to follow. Allow the dog to take the food as it moves forward, so reinforcing a 'bold' forward movement. Repeat this process a few times.

Then give your 'doggy' friends some pieces of food when they visit you and ask them to feed your dog when it comes up to them. Ask them not to touch the dog at all until it seems to be totally relaxed in the company of strangers.

Next introduce some touching, first of all on the dog's chest, gradually moving around the body, reinforcing the dog at the same time.

Repeat this with many people, before progressing to the stand for examination.

The stand for examination

The dog must stand in a show stance while the judge runs his or her hands over its body. The judge also examines the mouth to make sure the dog has the correct bite for its breed.

In obedience trials the handler must stand at varying distances in front of the dog while it is examined. At trials the mouth is not examined.

INITIAL CONDITIONING

If your dog won't stand and stay, you must teach this first, see exercise 5.
Enlist the help of a friend who has a good relationship with your dog to help with the initial conditioning.

1. Stand your dog at your left-hand side.

2. Ask your friend to approach the dog from the front but slightly towards the dog's left-hand side and walk past close to the dog. As your friend walks past, feed your dog a small piece of food.

3. Repeat point 2 a few times until the dog gets used to it.

4. Ask your friend to touch the dog briefly when passing it. Feed as this happens.

5. Gradually increase the amount of touching, but make sure that the dog never becomes stressed and avoids the hand.

6. Progress to a point where the dog can be examined fully, then feed *after* the examination is complete.

When your dog can be examined fully while it stands at your left-hand side, you can progress to the next stage.

7. Leave your dog in a stand stay position (exercise 5) and stand directly in front of your dog.

8. Ask your friend to examine your dog briefly. Feed as this happens.

9. Repeat point 8 once or twice.

10. Progress to a point where the dog can be examined fully, then reinforce *after* the examination is complete.

11. Gradually increase the distance between you and your dog until you have reached the standard you require.

MAINTAINING CONDITIONING

Reinforce the exercise intermittently.

The judging table

If your dog is frightened of the judging table, you can teach a happy response in a similar manner.

1. Feed the dog as it is picked up close to the table.
2. Feed the dog as it is placed on the table.

3. Repeat this act a few times before teaching the stand for examination on the table as recently described.

Heeling

Now that you have taught the dog to love being examined, I suggest you practise heeling as shown in exercise 6.

A good long run off the lead after the show, preferably with other friendly dogs, will help to convince your dog that going to shows is good fun.

Problems 6 and 7

Fear of, or aggression towards other dogs.

Remedy

Strange as it may seem, aggression is usually a reaction created by fear. Think about the times when you have been frightened. This usually occurs when you do not feel in control of a situation or when you are forced to do something which you do not really want to do. Therefore, generally speaking, we can use the same technique to overcome both fear and aggression in dogs. (Naturally, this does not include the few dogs who become aggressive through illness such as a brain tumour.)

In my experience, most dogs who show fear and associated aggression have not had the opportunity to meet other dogs when they were puppies, and so have never learnt good dog manners. Unfortunately if your dog is over four months old it will have missed

the best period for the development of canine social skills! However, do not give up. You can still help your dog to improve.

First of all, it would be best to stop going to dog shows for a while! In the meantime, take your dog out into as many different environments as practicable, preferably where it can meet other dogs off the lead. Leads, particularly short ones, are the direct cause of many acts of aggression as they do not allow dogs to relate to each other in a natural manner (see chapter 3).

Dogs need to sniff and smell one another in order to find out all sorts of social information. Imagine how you would feel if you held out your hand to greet someone, and the other person turned their back on you! This is probably what your dog feels when its type of social greeting is inhibited due to a tight lead.

Secondly, I would teach the stand stay (exercise 5)

or stand for examination as described earlier in this exercise. At the same time you can practice short bursts of heeling, making sure that the training is always an enjoyable experience for both you and the dog.

NOTE: Dogs who have shown aggression for a long time often require treatment from both a professional canine behaviourist and a veterinarian to try to cure the problem. First a detailed case history must be obtained from the owner to find out what triggers the aggression. Treatment to modify the dog's behaviour combined with possible desexing and drug therapy can then start under close supervision.

Problem 8

Boisterous uncontrolled behaviour in the ring.

Remedy
Boisterous uncontrolled behaviour is simply the result of lack of training. It can be remedied by teaching static exercises such as the stand, sit, drop and particularly the stay, see the relevant exercises earlier in this book. Essentially, when doing these exercises you are teaching controlled behaviour.

You must also make sure that your dog has regular daily exercise preferably off the lead so that it has the opportunity to experience different places and people and therefore becomes less excited by change. Taking your dog for walks will not only help to keep you fit but will increase your enjoyment of your pet.

I feel very strongly that the modern practice of forcibly 'stacking' dogs into an unnatural posture in the show ring should be discontinued. Experienced show handlers are able to hide, or minimise faults, by clever manipulation of the dog's stance and I cannot see the purpose of assessing conformation when the dog is held in this unnatural state. If one of the major purposes of showing is to select the best dogs for breeding, then surely the judges should insist that the dog is left to adopt a natural position so that they can get a true picture of the dog's composition. It would also assist them to assess the dog's temperament which in my view is just as important, if not more important, than the dog's anatomy.

It is also my belief that dogs should not be awarded Show Champion titles until they have been shown to be relatively free of any genetically inherited diseases which are common to their particular breed.

The dog should also be physically capable of carrying out the tasks for which it was originally bred.

EXERCISE *12* R̲E̲T̲R̲I̲E̲V̲I̲N̲G̲

The dog fetches an article and brings it back to the handler.

V̲ALUE OF RETRIEVING

1. It is an efficient and enjoyable way to exercise a dog, particularly if the owner cannot walk long distances.

2. It can be a source of entertainment to both you and your dog.

3. The dog learns to give up articles readily without the need for chasing or harassment. Dogs who run away with things can be a great source of frustration!

4. Retrieving is a useful preparation for other exercises, such as the seek back, tracking and scent discrimination.

5. The dog will be able to fetch and carry items such as the family newspaper.

6. It is an obedience trial requirement.

Creating an eagerness to retrieve

It is quite natural for many dogs to carry things around in their mouths. However, I have found in the training of thousands of dogs, that many show no natural inclination for this type of activity. This includes the retrieving breeds as well as those who are not recognised retrievers. First we need to explain how to overcome this particular problem for those people who have dogs like this. If your dog likes to pick up and hold articles you can go straight to the paragraph headed 'Initial conditioning'.

1. Find an article which your dog likes. It can be an old sock, slipper, rubber toy or just a piece of rag. I have found that many dogs like a piece of sheepskin.

2. Persuade the dog to mouth the article by either:
(a) holding it above its head and wriggling it, so encouraging the dog to jump up and grab it, or,
(b) scurrying the article along the ground, creating a desire to chase it.

NOTE: Do not wave or flick things into the dog's face. Always try to produce a bold forward movement towards the article.

3. When the dog mouths the article, pull on it in a gentle tug-of-war. Within a few seconds let the article go, allowing the dog to possess it. Repeat this several times.

4. Repeat point 3 but, this time, the instant your dog wins the article, run a short distance away in order to generate a desire in your dog to chase after you with the article in its mouth.

5. The instant the dog reaches you, hold on to the end of the article and have another gentle tug-of-war.

As a result of this game the dog will want to possess an article, hold it in its mouth, and bring it to you.

Owners of young dogs should be careful never to punish or scold their puppies for carrying forbidden articles in their mouths. Instead, remove items of value beyond the reach of that eager exploring mouth and leave it its own toys to play with. I believe many dogs have been discouraged from retrieving because, at a very impressionable age they have inadvertently been taught that it is naughty to pick things up.

Retrieving

INITIAL CONDITIONING

In common with most exercises, the best time to teach a dog to retrieve is when it is a puppy of eight to ten weeks old. The older the puppy grows without tuition, the less interest it will have in picking things up. Assuming your dog now enjoys holding an article, you can go on to the more formal act of retrieving.

1. Start with your dog near your left side. Throw an article about six paces away from you, making sure that it tumbles or bounces on landing to excite your dog's interest.

2. The moment your dog chases after the article, say the word 'fetch' and simultaneously move forward after it for a few paces.

3. When the dog has picked up the article, and not before, run away with your back to it thereby encouraging it to chase after you with the article in its mouth.

4. When the dog catches up with you, spin around quickly, dropping one hand, containing food, to its mouth, and putting the other hand under the article.

5. Say 'give' as the dog drops the article and reinforce it with a piece of food.

6. Repeat points 1–5 several times but not to a point where the dog appears bored.

MAINTAINING CONDITIONING

Gradually increase the distance you throw the article.
Reinforce intermittently as your dog's response becomes predictable.

SOME REFINEMENTS TO THE RETRIEVING EXERCISE

Retrieving on signal

If you intend to take part in obedience trials or club competitions, you will have to teach your dog to sit at your left-hand side while the article is thrown, and to retrieve only when the fetch signal is given. If you have followed the suggestions on teaching retrieving your dog should now be very eager to retrieve so it will be necessary to teach it to stay still while you throw the article.

1. Sit your dog at your left-hand side while holding the article in your right hand.

2. Signal your dog to 'wait' (stay) (see exercise 5) then gently pitch the article one pace in front of you. Your dog is unlikely to be stimulated by this action.

3. Step forward, pick up the article and return to your dog. Immediately reinforce your dog for remaining still.

4. Repeat points 1–3, gradually throwing the article further away from you.

5. Once the dog is quite steady when you throw the article, say 'fetch' after a few seconds' delay and simultaneously direct your dog towards the article by pointing enthusiastically towards it with your left arm.

6. As the dog returns with the article, reinforce immediately.

Sitting in front of the handler holding the article

For obedience trials you must also teach the dog to sit in front of you with the article in its mouth, and wait for the give signal before giving up the article. There are a number of ways of teaching this, depending on how keen your dog is to hold the article.

Method 1
I would suggest you try this method first.

As the dog returns with the article, move backwards for a few paces before coming to a quick halt and saying 'sit'. This will encourage the dog not only to sit close to you, but also, to look up. With its head in this position, the dog is more likely to keep holding the article in its mouth. Do not have food in your hand. When the dog sits, reinforce with food from your *pocket*.

Method 2
An alternative method is as follows:

As the dog returns with the article, turn 180 degrees and walk away signalling your dog to heel beside you (exercise 6). Take a few steps, then give the sit signal (exercise 2). Do not have food in your hand. When the dog sits at your left-hand side, instruct him to give the article, then reinforce with food from your *pocket*.

Repeat these actions a number of times, then progress to Method 1. Repeat Method 1 until it becomes unnecessary for you to move backwards to generate the sit response.

Method 3
Sit your dog in front of you. Offer it the article and, as it takes it in its mouth, say the word 'hold'. Before it attempts to drop the article say the word 'give' and take the article gently from its mouth. Reinforce immediately.

Repeat this process, gradually increasing the time between the hold and give signals. You can then use the voice signal 'hold' in conjunction with the hand signal 'sit' (exercise 2) to stimulate your dog to sit in front of you holding an article following a retrieve.

COMMON HANDLING PROBLEMS

When describing how to teach retrieving, I have mentioned how you can minimise the development of potential training problems. If you *do* find that you are experiencing any of the problems listed below, you will find that the remedy has already been covered earlier in this chapter.

1. The dog is not interested in chasing and holding an article.

2. The dog drops the article before reaching the handler.

NOTE: Some dogs develop the habit of holding onto the article and running away rather than giving it up to the handler. You will not encounter this problem if you use the M.I.D.I. method of training because your dog will *want* to give up the article so that it can take the food reinforcement.

RETRIEVING ON SIGNAL

THE STAY
Hand signal: Place your right hand in front of the dog's face.
Voice signal: Stay.

THE RETRIEVE
Hand signal: Point towards the article.
Voice signal: Fetch.

THE GIVE
Hand signal: Put your right hand under the dog's mouth.
Voice signal: Give.

EXERCISE *13* SEEK BACK

Your dog retraces your steps in order to find an article which you have dropped.

VALUE OF THE SEEK BACK

1. To find lost articles.
2. It is a preparation for teaching your dog to track or to do the scent discrimination exercise.
3. It is an obedience trial requirement.

The dog must learn to trace the lost article in fairly long grass using its sense of smell or the exercise is pointless. After all, if you drop something during a walk, it may be hundreds of metres away, making it impossible for the dog to find it using its eyes. Dogs who are taught on short grass generally use their eyes to sight the article and do not learn to follow a scent trail.

However, it is almost impossible for a dog to seek back by scenting in the polluted environment of an obedience trial ring, and these dogs primarily seek by using their eyesight.

Your dog must be a keen retriever before you attempt to teach the seek back exercise.

INITIAL CONDITIONING

Select a place which has not been walked over recently by other dogs or people with the grass about 10 cm high, or slightly shorter for small dogs. The article you use should be one which is familiar to the dog, and should carry your scent. A woollen glove is a good article to begin with.

Before starting to teach the exercise, get the dog to do a straight retrieve with your article once or twice, and reinforce the response.

1. Step off with your dog in the heeling position and your article in your right hand. Scuff the grass with your feet as you walk.

2. After several paces, drop the article, making this action obvious to the dog. Continue walking for a few more paces before doing an about-turn and directing your dog into a sit position.

3. Pause for a few seconds, then signal your dog to seek the article by making an animated hand signal which points along the track towards the article and saying 'fetch, seek' (see exercise 12). This will indicate to the dog that it is to bring an article back to you. Stimulate your dog to return to you as soon as the article is picked up by calling 'come'. Reinforce once the dog has given up the article.

4. Repeat the process on *fresh ground* gradually increasing the distance between the article and dog and phasing out the word 'fetch'. The voice signal 'seek' will then become associated with the act of finding an article by scenting.

As the response becomes predictable you can introduce further complexities into the exercise such as dropping the article surreptitiously, or laying a curved track, or a track with a right-angled turn. Use different everyday articles such as keys, wallet, spectacle case or address book.

MAINTAINING CONDITIONING

Reinforce the completed exercise intermittently, keeping training sessions short, successful and enjoyable.

COMMON HANDLING PROBLEMS

Problem
The dog is stimulated to pick up the article as soon as it is dropped during heeling.

Remedy
When you drop the article from your right hand, simultaneously offer food to the dog with your left hand. Continue walking for a few paces, then reinforce the dog for leaving the article on the ground. Repeat this procedure a few times, then gradually phase out the use of food for this purpose.

SEEK BACK

Hand signal: Point along the track towards the article with either arm.
Voice signal: Seek.

EXERCISE *14* SCENT DISCRIMINATION

Your dog seeks out and identifies a scented article belonging to you from amongst a group of articles, and brings it back to you.

VALUE OF SCENT DISCRIMINATION

1. It is a fun exercise to show off to friends and relatives! Scent discrimination is a relatively easy exercise to teach your dog because of its extraordinary sense of smell, yet other people will wonder how your dog can do it!

2. It is an obedience trial requirement.

INITIAL CONDITIONING

There are two ways to teach this exercise. The first is simple and successful as long as your dog does not become over-excited by retrieving, and you use the correct procedure.

The other way is more complex, but I believe it is more successful for excitable dogs. I suggest that you try the first method once or twice before deciding which one to use.

It is essential that you have taught your dog to retrieve (exercise 12) before you attempt this exercise.

You will need a few articles of similar shape, size and texture, e.g. four gloves, four key rings or four spectacle cases.

Handle one article from each group to give it your scent and do not touch any of the others except with tongs.

I will choose a glove for the following description.

NOTE: In obedience trials the articles which must be used are four rectangular strips of wood, four straps of leather and four tubular pieces of metal.

Method 1

As preparation, do a few ordinary retrieves with your scented glove and reinforce the correct response with food.

1. Place an unscented glove on the ground with a pair of tongs. Take up a position three or four paces from the article with your dog at your left-hand side.

2. Tell your dog to wait (exercise 5) and then throw your scented article so that it lands about 30 cms in front of the unscented one.

3. Send your dog with the voice signal 'seek' in conjunction with the same hand signal that you use for retrieving (exercise 12).

4. Reinforce immediately when your dog returns with the scented article.

5. Repeat this procedure, gradually throwing or placing your scented glove closer to the other one, and then beyond it.

6. When you are sure your dog will always retrieve the scented article, you can introduce the other similar unscented articles one at a time, placing them about 15 cms apart.

Throw or place your glove in various positions so that your dog has to use its nose to find the 'correct' one.

Up to this point your dog has been able to watch you place or throw the articles. You can now find out if the dog is, in fact, using its sense of smell to seek the article or whether it is picking it up because it has seen where it has landed.

7. Place yourself and your dog a few paces from the articles facing *away* from them. Ask an assistant to take your scented article in a pair of tongs and put it among the other articles.

8. Turn round, and send your dog to seek.

9. Reinforce immediately your dog returns with the scented article.

NOTE: In obedience trials the dog must sit in front of the handler before giving up the article (exercise 12).

Handlers of dogs who become very excited about retrieving may not be able to teach scent discrimination in this way. Their dogs may rush out and pick up the first article they come to without bothering about the variations in scent. These dogs can be taught by Method 2.

Method 2

You will notice from the instructions that follow that when using this method your dog will be taught to differentiate between smells before it leaves your side.

1. Choose two articles which are identical in shape, size and texture such as two gloves or two spectacle cases. Put your scent on one of these articles, but do not allow anyone to handle the other.

2. Hold the scented article in one hand and the other article in a pair of tongs.

3. Sit your dog in front of you and present the unscented article to your dog's face, preferably upright so that it is more likely to sniff it, than snatch it.

4. Before your dog can take this article, move it just out of reach.

5. Repeat points 2–4 a number of times until the dog makes no attempt to take the article.

6. Now, introduce your scented article and allow it to be sniffed. Let your dog take and hold the article for a few seconds before using the voice signal 'give' (exercise 12). Reinforce immediately.

7. Repeat this procedure a number of times, then give your dog a choice of articles. You can ask someone else to present the unscented article provided they know the routine.

8. Gradually present both articles closer to the ground until your dog finally makes its selection at ground level.

Now follow the instructions for Method 1 keeping your training sessions short and enjoyable.

COMMON HANDLING PROBLEMS

It is most important that you never punish your dog if it picks up the wrong article as this may confuse your dog and it may learn to dislike the whole exercise. Should it choose the wrong article, you should repeat the teaching procedure from the beginning in an environment which is free of distractions in order to reshape the behaviour you want.

SCENT DISCRIMINATION

Hand signal: Point towards the article with either arm.
Voice signal: Seek.

Portrait of Australia's native dog.

EXERCISE *15* DIRECTED RETRIEVE

The dog is required to retrieve one selected glove from a line of three gloves as shown in diagram 1.

This exercise is similar to the send away (exercise 19) in that the dog is taught to move out in a straight line, and will be of most interest to people who compete in obedience trials. However, there may be other dog-training enthusiasts who would like to learn it as part of their repertoire. Its practical use for the average dog-owner is limited.

Handlers who intend to compete in retrieving trials may find the exercise useful as it teaches the dog to move out in the direction of a hand signal.

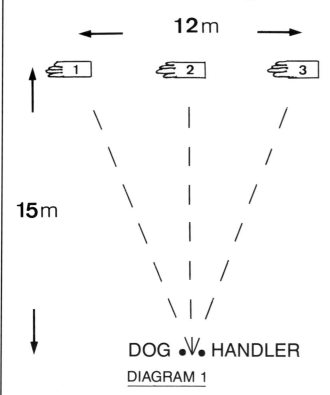

DIAGRAM 1

Three white gloves are placed 6 metres apart in a straight line. The handler and dog are positioned 15 metres from the gloves. The exercise starts with the dog and handler facing away from the gloves. The handler is directed by the Judge to send the dog to pick up a glove, either glove 1, 2, or 3. They about-turn and face the selected glove. The handler points

to the glove and gives a voice signal to retrieve (exercise 12).

If you have been teaching the exercises in the order presented in this book, then your dog will already have learnt to retrieve an article in a variety of ways:

- fetching a thrown article,
- seeking a dropped article,
- selecting your scented article from others.

During the directed retrieve, the gloves are not thrown, dropped or scented. They are simply placed in position at the commencement of the exercise and therefore the dog is unlikely to be motivated by the presence of white gloves lying on the ground some 15 metres away. Furthermore, there is nothing about the gloves to suggest to the dog that one glove is prefer-able to another. Consequently, when teaching this exercise we must begin by placing the gloves in a position which will guarantee success. I suggest you position them as shown in Diagram 2.

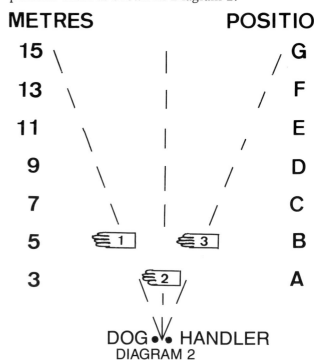

DIAGRAM 2

INITIAL CONDITIONING

1. Position yourself and your dog 3 metres from glove 2 in its position A. Place gloves 1 and 3 in position B. Tell the dog to stay (exercise 5) and place food under glove 2, making this action obvious to the dog. Return to the dog.

2. Send your dog to retrieve glove 2 by pointing to that glove with your left arm and giving the voice signal 'fetch'.

3. The moment the dog eats the food, say, 'fetch' again. Reinforce the dog when it brings back the correct glove. This second 'fetch' signal can gradually be phased out.

4. Move glove 2 to position B and repeat the above procedure a few times. The gloves are now in line.

5. Then move glove 2 to position C to teach the dog to retrieve at a greater distance, and also to ignore the other two gloves as he moves between them.

6. Now condition your dog with glove 2 at position D, and gloves 1 and 3 at position E.

7. Continue moving the gloves further away until you reach the 15 metre mark when all the gloves will be in line and 6 metres apart.

8. Repeat steps 1–7 with gloves 1 and 3. Start with glove 1 in position A and gloves 2 and 3 in position B and so on. This will teach your dog to follow the direction of your arm so that it will retrieve any one of the three gloves as directed.

MAINTAINING CONDITIONING

Eliminate food as a stimulus, i.e. the food under the glove, and intermittently reinforce with food after the dog has retrieved the correct article.

Obviously this exercise cannot be taught in one training session. Short bursts of training will quickly produce good results.

DIRECTED RETRIEVE

Hand signal: Point to the selected glove with your left arm.
Voice signal: Fetch.

EXERCISE 16 VISUAL SIGNAL EXERCISE

The dog learns to stand and stay beside the handler and to drop and sit at a distance from the handler, followed by a recall, then a return to heel. All these responses are elicited by visual hand signals only.

VALUE OF THE VISUAL SIGNAL EXERCISE

1. It controls the dog in an emergency when it may not be able to hear a voice signal, e.g. to stop it from crossing the road or getting into a dangerous situation.

2. It generates responses at a distance.

3. Teaching your dog to respond to visual signals will help you to communicate with it effectively if it becomes deaf later in life.

4. Teaching the visual signal exercise is a preparation for other exercises such as the send away (exercise 19) and stop on recall (exercise 21).

5. It is an obedience trial requirement.

We will deal with the various parts of this exercise in the order described at the beginning of the exercise.

Stand and stay on visual signal

It is not difficult to get your dog to stand (exercise 3) and stay (exercise 5) because the hand signals are given when the dog is beside you, and not at a distance. The dog should be well practised in these exercises before you try them without a voice signal. You may have to phase out the verbal signal gradually, but in my experience this is rarely necessary.

Problem

Sometimes a dog may move one or two steps forward after being signalled to stay.

Remedy

I suggest you get your dog to stand on a slight incline with its front feet higher than its back. Dogs are more likely to stand solidly in this position. Reinforce the appropriate response a few times, and then repeat the exercise on level ground.

Drop on visual signal

This part of the exercise offers a problem for many handlers. This may be due to the fact that dogs see the hand signal for drop (exercise 4) in a different way when they are facing their handlers instead of being beside them. For example, if you are facing your dog at a distance of a few paces and make a downward hand movement to signal your dog to drop, your dog may interpret this action as an encouragement to come to you because it is similar to the recall signal (exercise 1). Remember too, that a dog is excited by movement at ground level. It may therefore break from position instead of lying down.

I strongly recommend that you begin by teaching your dog to drop and sit at a distance on the *voice signals only*. A voice signal is much less likely to produce forward movement from the dog. Once it has thoroughly learnt the exercise with the voice signal you can introduce the hand signal at the same time. The next step is to phase out the voice signal until the dog is responding to the hand signal only.

This may appear to be a round-about way of teaching this exercise, but I can assure you that it will produce much more reliable results.

INITIAL CONDITIONING

At this stage in your training, your dog should drop immediately at your left-hand side when given the hand and voice signals (exercise 4).

1. Start with your dog sitting at your left-hand side. Get it to drop a number of times in the usual way, except make your hand signal less demonstrative each time, i.e. less of a downward movement. Your voice signal should be given fractionally before the modified hand signal. Then place your dog in a sit position facing you. Say 'Drop'. Sometimes a little body language, such as a slight knee bend can help to produce a quick drop response.

   Repeat this until the dog is dropping rapidly on the voice signal only. Reinforce the appropriate responses.

2. The same procedure should then be carried out starting with the dog in the stand position.

3. Leaving your dog in a stand position, move off one pace, about turn and face your dog. Say 'drop'. If your dog falters, use a little subtle body language to produce a rapid response. Reinforce the moment your dog lies down.

4. Repeat point 3 a number of times, gradually moving further away from your dog and reinforcing intermittently once the behaviour is conditioned.

5. Now introduce the hand signal with the voice signal, but make sure that your hand never drops low to the ground as in exercise 4. As discussed previously a low hand signal will tend to be interpreted by the dog as a signal to come to you. The hand signal should be given at the right side of your body from chest to hip level so that the dog can see it clearly at a distance.

6. Gradually phase out the voice signal, remembering to reinforce the dog when it drops quickly on the hand signal.

7. Practise this exercise at a variety of distances.

Sit from drop position on visual signal

Teach this exercise in the same way as teaching the drop from a stand position, i.e. teach the dog to respond to the voice signal only at first, then voice and hand signals together, and finally, the hand signal only.

1. Start with your dog at your left-hand side in a drop position. Get it to sit a number of times using both voice and hand signals (exercise 2) and reinforce. Gradually phase out the hand signal.

2. Now, stand in front of your dog who is in the drop position and say, 'sit'. If necessary, give a short upward hand signal at the right side of your body from waist level to shoulder level, but phase this out as soon as possible. Reinforce appropriate responses.

3. Repeat point 2, gradually moving further away from your dog and reinforcing intermittently once the behaviour is conditioned.

4. Now, introduce a hand signal in conjunction with the voice signal and gradually phase out the latter. The hand signal should be given at the right side of your body from waist level to head level so that the dog can see it clearly at a distance.

5. Practise at various distances away from your dog.

Recall and return to heel on visual signal

The recall and return to heel rarely offer problems provided that your dog is already well conditioned to respond to the voice and hand signals together (exercises 1 and 9). Simply phase out the voice signal gradually if this is necessary and reinforce the dog's response to the hand signal.

Important points about the visual signal exercise

It is most important that you avoid teaching these exercises in the same sequence all the time, otherwise the dog may learn to anticipate. For example you can stand and stay your dog, move off for a few paces and then return and reinforce the dog for remaining in that position. Alternatively you can practise another part of the exercise on its own.

When you do practise the whole sequence, I suggest you do it once or twice at the most, making sure that the dog is reinforced at different points of the sequence, e.g. after the drop or sit and not always when it has completed the exercise by returning to heel. Remember, you must keep the dog guessing which exercise is next and when it is going to be reinforced.

DROP ON VISUAL SIGNAL

Hand signal: Move your right hand from chest to hip level on the right side of your body.
Voice signal: None.

SIT FROM DROP ON VISUAL SIGNAL

Hand signal: Move your right hand from waist to head level on the right-hand side of your body.
Voice signal: None.

EXERCISE *17* JUMPING

The dog jumps over an obstacle on signal under the control of the handler.

VALUE OF JUMPING

1. It is a source of amusement for the handler and the dog.

2. It provides exercise.

3. The dog learns to negotiate objects such as creeks and fences and can be directed to jump into a car or utility.

4. It is an obedience trial requirement.

It is not natural for dogs to jump obstacles if left to their own devices because on many occasions jumping would not help them to survive in a natural environment, e.g. a dog might jump over an obstacle with a sharp drop on the other side. Consequently, you will see most untrained dogs going around or under a barrier rather than over it.

I have never found that teaching the jumping exercise makes a dog more likely to jump fences at home because the dog is taught to jump on signal, not of its own accord. A dog who has already learnt to jump out of his environment as a means of escaping boredom will probably continue to do so!

INITIAL CONDITIONING

I have already stated that it is not natural for a dog to jump over obstacles and we must remember this when teaching this exercise. We cannot expect the dog to jump until we have taught it that it is safe to do so as follows.

Put up an obstacle. The photographs illustrate a fairly elaborate set-up, similar to those used in obedience trials, but a piece of wood approximately 1½ metres long by 150 mm wide will do. Support the board on bricks or with stakes. The height of the jump should be very low at first, making it easy for the dog to negotiate.

Basically there are three different jumping procedures; sending over the jump, directing over the jump, or calling over the jump.

I use dry food when teaching this exercise as it is easier to manage.

Sending over the jump

1. Place your dog in the heel position at your left-hand side, approximately two paces from the jump and central to it.

2. Bring your right hand containing a piece of food to a point about 15 centimetres in front of the dog's face.

3. Thrust your right arm and hand forward, releasing the piece of food so that it goes over the centre of the jump and lands a few paces beyond it.

4. As the dog leaps after the food, give a voice signal such as 'over'. The act of jumping is instantly reinforced when the dog reaches the food.

5. Repeat points 1–4 several times, then move on to the next part of the exercise.

Directing over the jump

The only difference between sending over the jump and directing over the jump is that you will now stand *beside* the jump and direct the dog to leap by swinging your right hand and arm over the jump and, at the same time, saying 'over' (see the photograph). The dog is left in the same position central to the jump and food is utilised in the same way.

Calling over the jump

1. Leave your dog in a wait position (exercise 5), two or three paces from the centre of the jump.

2. Move around to the other side of the jump and take up a position opposite your dog but only one pace from the jump.

3. Extend your right hand, containing food, towards your dog and say 'come'.

4. The moment your dog moves towards the jump say, 'over' and step back quickly to give your dog space to land. Reinforce immediately.

5. Repeat several times, gradually placing yourself two or three paces from the jump and making your hand signal less demonstrative.

Jumping over a series of obstacles

Teach your dog to jump each obstacle as in 'sending over the jump' before progressing to this stage. Place your low obstacles in a line.

1. Walk towards the first obstacle with your dog in the heel position so that it is approaching the centre of the jump.

2. When you are two paces from the jump, give the voice signal over, and thrust your left arm forward towards the jump.
NOTE: It is easier to use a left hand signal when you are moving past a series of obstacles.

3. Quickly move around the side of the jump as your dog jumps over the centre of it.

4. Reinforce the dog once it has jumped.

5. Approach the other jumps in the same manner.

MAINTAINING CONDITIONING

Do this in the usual way, making sure that your dog is enjoying the exercise all the time. It is important to realise that the obstacles should never be placed at a height which overfaces the dog and puts it off.

You can progress to a point where the dog will run through an obstacle course without being given any signals.

SENDING OVER THE JUMP

Hand signal: Thrust your right arm forward towards the jump.
Voice signal: Over.

CALLING OVER THE JUMP

Hand signal: Extend your right arm towards the jump, then draw your hand back towards your waist.
Voice signal: Over.

DIRECTING OVER THE JUMP

Hand signal: Swing your right arm over the jump.
Voice signal: Over.

JUMPING OVER A SERIES OF OBSTACLES

Hand signal: Thrust your *left* arm forward towards the jump.
Voice signal: Over.

Highflyer!

EXERCISE 18 DIRECTIONAL JUMPING

The dog is placed between two jumps and directed to jump over one of them.

If you think about the exercises you have taught your dog so far, you will realise that all of them have conditioned the dog to return straight to you, e.g. the recall, retrieving, etc. Teaching a dog to move to the right or left on signal helps you control it. For instance, if your dog gets on the other side of a fence during a walk, you can signal it to move to the right or left to find an opening and return to you. I usually teach a dog to deviate on signal by teaching directional jumping. Obviously the dog must have already been taught jumping (exercise 17).

Equipment

You will need two low jumps, and two small discs on which to place food, so that the food is obvious to the dog. You may need the help of another person, if your dog is not very good at staying (exercise 5).

Put up two jumps parallel to each other about three to four paces apart. Place a small white disc of 50 mm diameter on the far side of each jump, approximately two to three paces from the centre of each jump. The dog must be able to see the discs easily, as illustrated in the photograph.

INITIAL CONDITIONING

Start with low jumps so that the dog can see the discs clearly and can negotiate the jumps easily.

1. Heel your dog to a position midway between the jumps and direct it to sit.

2. Wait your dog (exercise 5), step off two or three paces directly in front of your dog then turn and face it.

3. Either:
   (a) Ask an assistant to place food on the left-hand disc, or
   (b) Move around the jump and place it in position yourself as shown in the photograph. Make sure the dog sees the food being placed on the disc. This will make it jump in the direction of the disc when given the signal. Return to the position facing your dog.

4. Direct your dog to jump by offering a wide arm signal with your left arm pointing at the jump and simultaneously saying 'over'. The act of jumping in that direction will be instantly reinforced when the dog reaches the food.

5. Immediately call your dog to you around the side of the jump and reinforce again.

6. Repeat points 1–5 a few times, then follow the same procedure using the right-hand disc and a right arm signal.

7. Gradually begin to direct the dog first over one jump then the other so that the dog learns to follow the direction indicated by the hand signal.

MAINTAINING CONDITIONING

Eventually the discs should be removed and the dog should be intermittently reinforced on successful completion of the exercise.

Then move the jumps further and further apart and place yourself further away from the dog. It may be necessary to use the discs and food again at this time but phase them out as soon as the dog's response is predictable.

The height of the jump can be increased once food is no longer required.

DIRECTIONAL JUMPING

Hand signal: Swing your arm from waist level in the direction in which you want the dog to jump.
Voice signal: Over.

EXERCISE 19 THE SEND AWAY AND DIRECTED JUMPING

The handler sends the dog away from the stand position to a point at least 6 metres beyond the jumps. On signal, it is required to turn and sit, and is then directed over a nominated jump. The exercise is repeated with the dog required to jump the other obstacle.

Competitors at obedience trials are required to perform the send away exercise followed by the directed jump as illustrated in Diagram 1.

In some countries, such as New Zealand, the send away is an exercise in its own right without jumping, but the dog is required to go a long distance from the handler. This ability is of value to handlers and dogs who take part in field or retrieving trials.

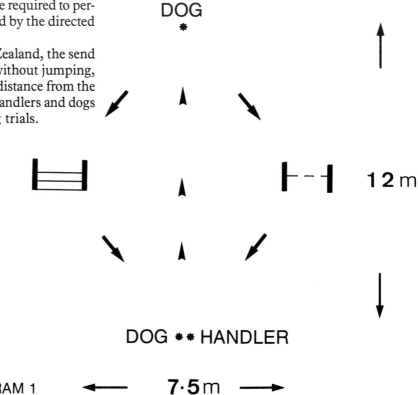

DOG

12 m

DOG ** HANDLER

DIAGRAM 1 ← 7·5 m →

The send away
INITIAL CONDITIONING

Your dog must be thoroughly conditioned to the visual signal sit (exercise 16) before you attempt the send away.

1. Leave your dog in a sit stay position (exercise 5). Place a small white disc on the ground a few paces in front of the dog. Put food on the disc. The dog should watch this process so that it runs towards the disc when the signal is given. Return to your dog.

2. Send your dog with an animated left-hand signal which points towards the disc together with the voice signal 'go' or 'away'. Your dog will go to the disc and be immediately reinforced with food.

3. The moment your dog eats the food, attract its attention by calling its name. As the dog turns around, give the hand and voice signals to sit (exercise 16). Go to the dog and reinforce that response.

4. Repeat points 1–3, gradually increasing the distance between you and disc until it is approximately 12 metres away.

MAINTAINING CONDITIONING

Ask an assistant to place food on the disc occasionally. Eventually remove the disc completely but always go to your dog immediately it has sat down and reinforce intermittently until you are ready to teach the directed jumping.

THE SEND AWAY

Hand signal: Swing your left arm forward, so that it points in the relevant direction.
Voice signal: Go or Away.

THE SIT

Hand signal: Move your right hand from waist to head level on the right hand side of your body.
Voice signal: Sit.

Directed jumping

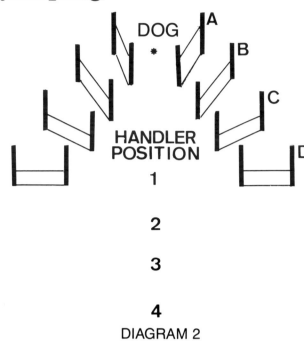

DIAGRAM 2

There are some fundamental differences between what I have called directional jumping (exercise 18) and the directed jumping associated with the send away in obedience trials. The main difference lies in the position of the dog relative to the jumps, and in the position of the jumps themselves. In the former, the jumps are placed parallel to one another and the dog sits between them, while in the latter, the jumps are placed in line with each other and the dog sits beyond them. It will be much easier for you to teach this exercise if you have already taught directional jumping.

It is important to arrange your equipment so that you can produce a successful response every time you ask your dog to jump. Diagram 2 shows how you can do this. Setting the jumps at the angles shown, and gradually advancing to the point where you can jump your dog when the jumps are in line, will also minimise the possibility of your dog going around a jump instead of over it.

INITIAL CONDITIONING

Arrange the jumps as illustrated in Diagram 2 starting with them in position A. The jumps should be very low at this stage.

1. Place your dog in a sit position between the jumps and say 'wait' (exercise 5). Move off six paces, about turn and face your dog so you are in handler position 1. You will notice that this arrangement is very like directional jumping.

2. Ask an assistant to place a piece of food on a disc on the other side of one of the jumps making this action obvious to the dog, or move around the jump and place it in position yourself.

3. Return to position 1 and signal your dog to jump. The moment your dog lands and eats the food, call it to you and reinforce again. Repeat this a number of times using both jumps in an unpredictable pattern so that your dog does not begin to anticipate the direction of the jump.

4. Now place your dog in its original position with the jumps at angle B. Place yourself in position 2 and repeat the procedure in point 3.

5. Continue conditioning in a similar way moving the jumps to position C and finally to position D, while you take up position 3 and finally position 4.

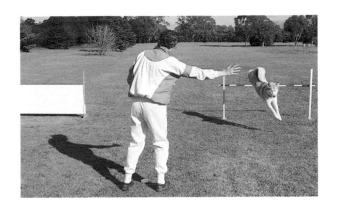

At this point, you, the dog and the jumps will be in the positions required by the rules in obedience trials (see diagram 1) i.e.:
- the jumps will be 7.5 metres apart and in line with one another,
- your dog will start the exercise sitting 6 metres beyond the line of the jumps and central to them,
- you will be 6 metres in front of the jumps and central to them.

The jump height can be gradually increased to the required level.

MAINTAINING CONDITIONING

Eliminate food as a stimulus and reinforce with food intermittently.

Combining the send away and directed jump

You can now combine the two exercises already described. Start with the dog being sent away to a disc with food on it, the jumps in position A and the handler in position 1. Common sense will tell you how quickly you can progress.

Problems may occur if you practise for too long, jump your dog over high jumps frequently, or try to progress too quickly. Remember, too, that your dog must be eager for its food reinforcement at all training sessions.

DIRECTED JUMPING

Hand signal: Swing your arm from waist level in the direction you want your dog to jump.
Voice signal: Over.

EXERCISE 20 RETRIEVE OVER THE HIGH JUMP

The dog must sit and wait beside you in the heel position while you throw an object over a jump. (In Obedience Trials the object must be a wooden dumbbell.) On a signal, the dog is required to jump the obstacle, pick up the object, and return to you by jumping back over the obstacle. It should then sit in front of you holding the object, give it up on signal, and then return to the heel position on signal.

Retrieving (exercise 12) and jumping (exercise 17) have already been taught. We now have to combine the two.

VALUE OF RETRIEVE OVER THE HIGH JUMP

This exercise has little practical value in everyday life except for gun dogs who may be required to negotiate a barrier when retrieving game. It is a fun exercise which most dogs thoroughly enjoy and is also an obedience trial requirement.

Before starting to teach the retrieve over the high jump there are one or two points to consider in order to ensure rapid conditioning. First of all, the ground should be firm, but slightly yielding. Grass is best. Secondly, the jump height must be very low at first so that the dog can easily see the object as it lands.

INITIAL CONDITIONING

1. Place yourself and your dog just far enough away from a low jump to allow for a good take off. If you start off too far away, the dog may run around the jump to pick up the article.

2. Wait your dog (exercise 5), then throw the article over the jump so that it lands central to the jump and only a few paces away from it.

3. Pause a few seconds, then send your dog to retrieve by thrusting your right arm forward towards the jump and saying 'over', or 'fetch', or both. While the dog is picking up the article, step forward towards the jump. As the dog turns towards you with the article in its mouth, extend your right arm over the centre of the jump to draw your dog to you and say 'over' again. Step back rapidly as the dog approaches the jump to give it plenty of room to land.

4. Signal the dog to sit in front of you with the article in its mouth for a few seconds before asking it to give (exercise 12, retrieving on signal).

5. Repeat points 2–4 gradually throwing your article further away from the jump. Phase out the hand and voice signal as the dog jumps back over the jump so that your dog jumps, retrieves and returns to you over the jump on the first hand and voice signal. Position yourself further away from the jump, so that your dog has plenty of space to land without you having to move backwards.

When a dumbbell is used, it should be thrown so that it doesn't bounce outwards to either side of the jump. After the retrieve the dog will probably return directly to you without jumping, if this happens. It is easier to throw the dumbbell accurately if you hold it by one end, toss it forward, and at the same time flick it so that it tends to rotate backwards through the air and stop on landing. Practise a few times without the dog.

The speed with which you raise the jump height is largely a matter of common sense. I see little point in jumping dogs to test their agility to extreme.

MAINTAINING CONDITIONING

Dogs trained in the M.I.D.I. way find this activity enjoyable in its own right, but the occasional food reinforcement will ensure that you maintain effective conditioning.

RETRIEVE OVER THE HIGH JUMP

Hand signal: Thrust your right arm forward towards the jump.
Voice signal: Fetch.

EXERCISE *21* STOP ON RECALL

The dog is left in a sit, wait position. It is required to stop promptly on a voice and hand signal after being called to come towards you. When the dog has stopped, after a short pause it is called to sit in front of you, and then directed into the heel position.

I mentioned this exercise in the visual signal exercise (exercise 16). Once again it is easier if you first teach a response to a voice signal and then introduce the hand signal.

VALUE OF STOP ON RECALL

1. To stop the dog in an emergency, e.g. if the dog is in danger of running out in front of a car.

2. To bring the dog to a halt at a distance.

3. General control.

4. It is an obedience trial requirement.

NOTE: Obedience trials require that the dog specifically *drops* on recall. I believe the emphasis should be placed on the dog stopping in any position because this is more likely to ensure the dog's survival in an emergency. For this reason you should practise this exercise when your dog is running towards you in play so that it learns to respond in an everyday situation.

However, when teaching this exercise, I shall follow on from the visual signal exercise routine (exercise 16) where the dog is dropped from the stand position at a distance.

INITIAL CONDITIONING

Your dog must be thoroughly conditioned to drop from the stand position at a distance before you attempt this exercise.

1. Practise the drop from a stand position once or twice, using the *voice signal* 'drop' only and reinforce successful responses.

2. Leave your dog in a stand wait position (exercise 5), walk away five paces and turn to face your dog.

3. Call your dog to you but, the moment it moves, give it the voice signal to drop. Return to the dog and reinforce the correct response.

4. Repeat points 2 and 3 gradually increasing the distance between you and the dog, and allowing the dog to make more movement towards you before offering the voice signal 'drop'. Continue to return to your dog and reinforce it in the drop position.

5. Once the drop on voice signal has been thoroughly taught, you can make a hand signal in conjunction with the verbal signal. This signal should be made at the right side of the body with the hand going from chest to hip level. This will allow the dog to see the signal at a distance without confusing it with a straight recall. Remember, if your visual signal goes close to the ground, this action may stimulate your dog to come straight to you.

MAINTAINING CONDITIONING

When the dog drops every time on signal as it comes towards you, you can then start calling your dog to sit in front of you to complete the set exercise. However, the drop response should continue to be reinforced intermittently.

It is important to vary this exercise otherwise the dog may begin to anticipate the drop signal. To help the dog understand whether you require a straight recall or a drop on recall, I suggest you offer slightly different signals for the recall before the drop, and the recall after the drop, as shown in the box.

DROP ON RECALL

THE RECALL BEFORE THE DROP
Leave the dog in a sit position.
Hand signal: Extend both arms towards your dog then draw them towards your waist.
Voice signal: Come.

THE DROP
Hand signal: Move your right hand from chest to hip level on the right side of your body.
Voice signal: Drop.

THE RECALL AFTER THE DROP
Hand signal: Drop your right hand low to the ground.
Voice signal: Come.

EXERCISE 22 BARK ON SIGNAL

The dog barks on a hand and/or voice signal, in a sit, stand and drop position.

VALUE OF BARK ON SIGNAL

1. It is useful for personal defence or home security.

2. It is currently an obedience trial requirement.

It can be difficult to live with a dog that barks at anything and everything. However, a dog that rarely barks can be a disappointment to people who would like their dog to frighten away potential burglars. You can have the best of both worlds, that is, a dog which does not annoy the neighbours, but which sounds like a trained guard dog when required!

Although I am totally opposed to training dogs to attack, because I believe this makes their behaviour unnaturally aggressive and unpredictable, I can see no problem in pretending that your dog will protect your property! 'Beware of the dog' signs are a good deterrent. Saying 'don't touch' to your dog when you answer the door to a stranger will probably make a potential intruder think twice about his plans. A subtle signal which makes your dog bark will certainly conjure up images of possible attack and injury. Little do people realise that your dog is more likely to lick them in friendship!

Incidentally, a dog which is left inside the house when you go out, will act as a more efficient deterrent to would-be housebreakers than one which is left outside, because they cannot gauge what the dog's reaction will be if they enter the home.

INITIAL CONDITIONING

Let us assume that your dog barks occasionally.

1. Place yourself beside your dog when it starts to bark.

2. When the dog barks, instantly give the voice signal 'speak' in conjunction with a small hand signal. This is usually a hand movement that mimics the opening of the dog's mouth as it barks.

3. Reinforce the dog.

4. Try to anticipate the next bark by watching your dog's body language. Give the voice and hand signal just *before* it barks.

5. Reinforce instantly when the dog barks.

6. Repeat points 4 and 5 on a few occasions until your dog becomes conditioned to your signals.

NOTE: It may be better for you to teach your dog to respond to a very subtle signal if you want it to bark on signal for protection. You could snap your fingers or scratch your ear or use any other gesture which the intruder wouldn't recognise as a signal for your dog to bark.

MAINTAINING CONDITIONING

Reinforce the response intermittently as usual.

BARK ON SIGNAL

Hand signal: Point your right hand towards your dog and open it in a way that mimics a dog's mouth when barking.
Voice signal: Speak.

EXERCISE 23 FOOD REFUSAL

Your dog learns to leave food alone, when you indicate that it should do so.

VALUE OF FOOD REFUSAL

1. You can tell your dog not to eat food which is lying on the ground. This helps the dog survive if it is about to help itself to things like cooked chicken bones or something poisonous like snail bait.

2. It teaches manners at meal times because your dog can be taught to sit and wait for the signal to eat.

This means that a small child or elderly person can feed the dog without the danger of being bowled over.

3. It is currently an obedience trial requirement.

NOTE: People often think that this exercise will teach the dog not to take a bait. Be warned, this is not true.

INITIAL CONDITIONING

1. Place an empty dish on the ground.

2. Holding a piece of food in your right hand, heel your dog up to the dish, off lead (exercise 6). As you reach it tell the dog to 'stand, leave', and immediately reinforce with the food from your hand. If the dog looks down at the dish, make a rapid gesture with your right hand to stimulate it to look up at you. Feed the dog immediately.

3. Heel your dog away from the dish the moment it has swallowed the reinforcement using an exaggerated hand signal (exercise 6). Reinforce again after taking a few steps.

4. Repeat points 2 and 3 a few times. The dog will gradually become conditioned to the idea that leaving the dish alone is of benefit to it.

5. Now repeat points 2 and 3 again after placing a few pieces of boring food such as diced carrots or dry food in the dish. Heel away from the dish using *meat* as a stimulus, then reinforce. Repeat several times.

6. Finally place meat or bones in the dish. Be alert for the slightest movement from your dog which would indicate an interest in the food in the dish. Continue to use meat as a stimulus to heel the dog away from the dish a few times. Gradually phase this out and use the meat as an intermittent reinforcement after the successful completion of the food refusal exercise.

You can vary the exercise in the following way. The first variation is useful at meal times.

Sit or stand your dog and say 'wait'. Place a dish of food in front of your dog saying 'leave'. Pause for a few seconds before signalling the dog to eat by pointing at the dish and saying 'yours' or 'eat' or whatever word you favour.

Another variation is currently required at obedience trials. The dog is left in the sit, stand or drop position. The handler steps off five paces and halts with his or her back to the dog. Food is then offered to the dog by an assistant, either by hand or in a dish. After a few seconds the food is removed and the handler is instructed to return to the dog.

▌INITIAL CONDITIONING

1. Sit your dog at your left-hand side. Give the hand and voice signal for stay (exercise 5). Ask an assistant to place an empty dish in front of your dog. As this happens say 'leave' and simultaneously give your dog a piece of fresh meat. Ask your assistant to remove the dish.

2. Repeat point 1 with boring food such as diced carrots.

3. Repeat point 1 putting fresh meat or bones in the dish.

4. Sit your dog at your left-hand side. Give the hand and voice signal for stay. Ask an assistant to place a dish of meat or bones in front of your dog. Say 'leave', pause for a few seconds, then ask your assistant to remove the dish. Reinforce your dog immediately *after* the successful completion of the exercise.

➡

5. Sit your dog at your left-hand side. Place your right hand in front of the dog's face and say 'stay, leave'. Take one step forward in front of your dog keeping your back to it. Ask your assistant to place an empty dish in front of your dog. After a few seconds the assistant should remove the dish. Step back to your dog and reinforce immediately with fresh meat.

6. Repeat point 5 with boring food.

7. Repeat point 5 with fresh meat or bones. Your assistant must be quick to remove the dish of food if the dog looks as if it is going to take the food.

8. Repeat points 5–7 gradually moving further from the dish.

MAINTAINING CONDITIONING

Reinforce the completed exercise intermittently.

NOTE: In obedience trials, competitors are not allowed to use the word 'leave' and the exercise must be carried out in the sit, stand and drop positions.

COMMON HANDLING PROBLEMS

When teaching exercises the M.I.D.I. way it is most important to anticipate and prevent any undesirable or unwanted behaviour in your dog. This is particularly important with the food refusal exercise as your dog will be inadvertently reinforced if it eats the food in the dish. To make sure this does not occur, pay particular attention to the following points:

1. During initial conditioning always leave the dish beyond easy reach of the dog.

2. Let the dog know that you are carrying the more desirable food, i.e. meat.

3. Stimulate your dog to move away from the dish using very exaggerated hand signals.

4. Watch your dog's body language very carefully so that you can pre-empt any action to grab the food.

Never say 'leave' or make other signals in an aggressive manner. This could result in bizarre behaviour such as fear responses towards the dish.

FOOD REFUSAL

(dog and handler beside dish)

Hand signal: Place your right hand in front of the dog's face.
Voice signal: Stand, leave.

FOOD REFUSAL

(obedience trials)

Hand signal: Place your right hand in front of the dog's face.
Voice signal: Stay.